THE ART OF
PROPHECY

THE ART OF PROPHECY

AUTHORED BY THE GREAT PROPHETS AND ARTISTS

WORKING UNDER THE DIRECTION OF GOD

COMPILED BY JACK B. SCHARR

WITH ART COMMENTARY BY ANGELIA HAYES

FINE ART LTD.   ST. LOUIS, MISSOURI

ISBN NUMBER 0-970368607

LIBRARY OF CONGRESS CARD CATALOG NUMBER 00-107655

PRINTED IN HONG KONG

DESIGNED BY CAROL HARALSON

SPECIAL THANKS TO DAN HOLDER, WAYNE CARSON,

JAKE ROSEN, CAROLYN CARSON, GAIL TUSMAN,

LINDA MORRIS, JACK O'GRADY, AND DEBRA SCHARR.

PAGE ONE AND ENDSHEETS

Dante's Divine Comedy, early 15th century
Yates Thompson 36 f. 141, The Mystery of the Redemption
British Library, London, UK/Bridgeman Art Library

PAGE SIX

Gentile da Fabriano (1385–1427)
Nativity, Part of the predella, from the altarpiece of the Adoration of the Magi (Strozzi Altarpiece), 1423
Uffizi, Florence, Italy/Nicolo Orsi Battaglini/Art Resource, NY

PAGE TWO

This painting has been attributed to Albrecht Dürer and bears his monogram
Madonna of the Cherries
Collection of Nicholas and Sophia Karakas, St. Louis, Missouri

In *Madonna of the Cherries,* multiple themes from the gospel are represented through the use of iconography. The artist depicts the Christ child holding fruit in one hand and a butterfly in the other. The three cherries are used to represent the trinity; however, the fruit, which ripens only to wither, then die, symbolizes man's mortality. The trinity can never die but man will. Conversely, the butterfly represents the immortality man can achieve through the divinity of Christ. Like Christ, the butterfly is entombed and emerges reborn from its cocoon. Christ, who embodies both the human and the divine, is the key to man's rebirth and resurrection.

CONTENTS

PREFACE   7

THE PROPHECIES   10

AFTERWORD   212

BIBLIOGRAPHY   214

INDEX TO ARTWORKS   214

PREFACE

Is the Bible truly the word of God, or is it a compilation of random writings from people throughout history? We believe God inspired many to write the Bible, but that its words are God's alone.

As we studied Old Testament prophecies concerning the last two thousand years, we were astonished at how many had come to fruition. From foretellings of the life, death, and resurrection of Christ to those concerning other historical events and developments, we found hundreds of prophecies that had come to fulfillment. As you examine the prophecies and study the paintings in the pages that follow, we think you will agree that such a clear relationship between prophecy and outcome could not be the result of random chance, but truly a demonstration of the fulfillment of the word of God.

> Above all, you must understand that no prophecy of Scripture came about by the prophet's own interpretation. For prophecy never had its origin in the will of man, but men spoke from God as they were carried along by the Holy Spirit.
>
> —— 2 PETER 1:20-21

Prophecies, both in the Old and New Testament, are written so that when the things prophesied come to pass we will know they are from God. In John 13:19, Jesus said of prophecy: "I am telling you now, before it happens, so that when it does happen, you will believe that I am He."

In this book we present the astonishing fulfillment of prophecy from the Old Testament into the New Testament, or since the completion of the New Testament. Hundreds of prophecies have been fulfilled; we have included the ones we felt were most important. Likewise there are thousands of existing artworks based on biblical figures and events. We have chosen some of the most inspiring, and inspired, from among them to illuminate this book.

In filling the pages of *The Art of Prophecy* with the glories of the painted Word, we follow in the footsteps of early Christians who taught and testified through painted images. Gutenberg invented a successful printing press in 1455 and the first books he produced were two hundred Bibles. But prior to that, the contents of the Bible were conveyed to the people by priests and rabbis reading from hand-duplicated scrolls and by the inspiring presence of religious paintings, sculpture, and architecture. The ability to read and write was confined to a scant number of nobles, priests, and scribes, so it was the job of the artist to present the Bible visually to the people.

These early artists created a visual text of the Bible, including the word of God. *The Art of Prophecy* presents many of their greatest masterpieces along with commentary about their inspiration, sources, and meanings, as interpreted by art historians and our own art consultants. We combine these great paintings with the Bible prophecies and fulfillments upon which they were based. To show how prophecy is still being fulfilled today, we present the works of the old masters as they relate to modern day prophecy fulfillment.

We have paired works by many of the world's most beloved artists with two thousand years of fulfilled prophecy from the Bible. We hope this union will inspire all who turn these pages.

> *Do not think that I have come to abolish the Law or the Prophets; I have not come to abolish them but to fulfill them. I tell you the truth, until Heaven and earth disappear, not the smallest letter, not the least stroke of a pen, will by any means disappear from the Law until everything is accomplished.*
> —— MATTHEW 5:17-18, C AD 28

Note: The Bible verses we have used are taken from the New International Version (NIV) of the Bible. We have included dates with most of the verses. These dates reflect the approximate year in which the words reported in scripture were actually spoken, or the event being recorded took place.

GENTILE DE FABRIANO (1385-1427)
The Adoration of the Magi, 1423

Uffizi, Florence, Italy. Scala/Art Resource, NY

An example of the place of prophecy in art is Gentile de Fabriano's Nativity. The artist has given us a plethora of imagery in this altarpiece. The left hand arc shows the three kings as they see the star for the first time. The middle arc places the magi and their massive entourage on the road to Bethlehem and in the right arc, they are entering the city. In the foreground we see the eldest king kneeling down, crown removed, receiving Christ's blessing. Behind him the second king removes his crown. The youngest king waits his turn, as his servant removes his spurs. Mary's midwives are entranced with one of the vases containing the holy gifts. (The holy gifts which were prophesied 1250 years earlier!) The upper section of the altarpiece contains three roundels. The center roundel reveals the Lord's blessing representing the new covenant. The left and right roundels illustrate the annunciation, and each is framed by reclining prophets. The left side of the predella of the altarpiece presents us with another nativity scene. Here the Holy Family sits alone prior to the arrival of the Magi. The center depicts the flight to Egypt, then the presentation in the temple.

CHRIST WILL COME BEFORE THE DESTRUCTION OF THE TEMPLE

OLD TESTAMENT PROPHECIES

After the sixty-two 'sevens,' the Anointed One will be cut off and will have nothing. The people of the ruler who will come will destroy the city and the sanctuary. The end will come like a flood: War will continue until the end, and desolations have been decreed. — DANIEL 9:26, C 535 BC

NEW TESTAMENT FULFILLMENT

After three days they found him in the temple courts, sitting among the teachers, listening to them and asking them questions. Everyone who heard him was amazed at his understanding and his answers. — LUKE 2:46-47, C AD 6-12

The temple in Jerusalem was totally destroyed in 70 A.D. according to Daniel's writing. The Anointed One must appear and be cut off (crucified) before the destruction of the temple. Jesus entered the temple, and later told of its future destruction.

DUCCIO DI BUONINSEGNA (C. 1278-1318)

Maesta: Disputation with the Doctors, 1308-11

Museo dell'Opera del Duomo, Siena, Italy/Bridgeman Art Library

Christ began teaching at the age of twelve. In this image Duccio narrates that first teaching in the temple. The elders sit in amazement while they listen to the wisdom of this child. On the left a panicked Mary and Joseph enter the temple to reunite with their son who has been separated from them.

CHRIST BORN OF A WOMAN REDEEMS THE WORLD FROM ORIGINAL SIN

OLD TESTAMENT PROPHECY

And I will put enmity between you and the woman, and between your offspring and hers; he will crush your head, and you will strike his heel. — GENESIS 3:15, IN THE BEGINNING

NEW TESTAMENT FULFILLMENT

But when the time had fully come, God sent his Son, born of a woman, born under law to redeem those under law that we might receive the full rights of sons.

— GALATIANS 4:4, C AD 58

There is poetic justice in God using a woman, specifically a virgin, to reverse the effects of the original sin. This woman brings forth the Redeemer who will thoroughly vanquish the evil one. The evil one strikes the Redeemer's heel [the crucifixion of Christ] but Christ's resurrection renders this wound a minor one.*
*redeem=to buy back.

MICHELANGELO BUONARROTI (1475-1564)

Detail from The Original Sin and the Expulsion from Paradise, 1508-1512

Sistine Chapel, Vatican Palace, Vatican State. Scala/Art Resource, NY

In Michelangelo's painting, the tree with its branches outstretched takes on the form of a cross. This is to make explicit the connection between Adam and Christ. Christ is the new Adam. Man's fall (the fall of Adam) will be transformed by the new Adam, Christ, into redemption and ultimately salvation. The Tree of Knowledge is therefore connected directly to the cross.

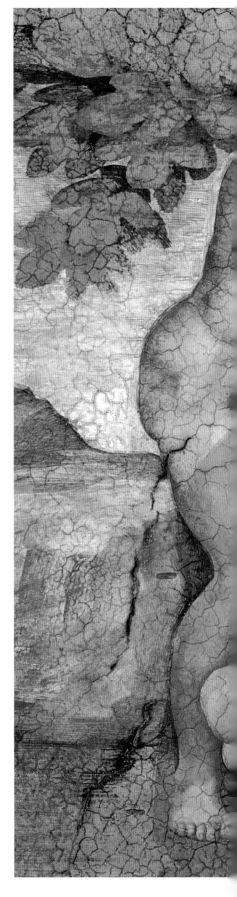

MARY IS TOLD THAT SHE WILL GIVE BIRTH TO THE SON OF GOD

NEW TESTAMENT PROPHECY

In the sixth month, God sent the angel Gabriel to Nazareth, a town in Galilee, to a virgin pledged to be married to a man named Joseph, a descendant of David. The virgin's name was Mary. The angel went to her and said, "Greetings, you who are highly favored! The Lord is with you." Mary was greatly troubled at his words and wondered what kind of greeting this might be. But the angel said to her, "Do not be afraid, Mary, you have found favor with God. You will be with child and give birth to a son, and you are to give him the name Jesus. He will be great and will be called the Son of the Most High. The Lord God will give him the throne of his father David, and he will reign over the house of Jacob forever; his kingdom will never end." "How will this be," Mary asked the angel, "since I am a virgin?" The angel answered, "The Holy Spirit will come upon you, and the power of the Most High will overshadow you. So the holy one to be born will be called the Son of God. Even Elizabeth your relative is going to have a child in her old age, and she who was said to be barren is in her sixth month."

— LUKE 1:26-36, C 6-2 BC

NEW TESTAMENT FULFILLMENT

While they were there, the time came for the baby to be born, and she (Mary) gave birth to her firstborn, a son. She wrapped him in cloths and placed him in a manger, because there was no room for them in the inn. — LUKE 2:6-7, C 6-2 BC

JAN VAN EYCK (C. 1390-1441)

The Ghent altarpiece, closed state: Annunciation, Prophets Zaccariah and Micah, Eritrean and Cumean Sibyls, Donors, Saints John the Baptist and John the Evangelist, 1432

Cathedral St. Bavo, Ghent, Belgium. Scala/Art Resource, NY

Van Eyck's version of the Annunciation is rich in symbolism pointing directly to Christ's coming as the fulfillment of Old Testament prophecy. In the niches above the angel Gabriel and Mary are the prophets Zechariah and Micah, and the sibyls Cumean and Eritrean, holding scrolls inscribed with the prophecies foretelling Christ's coming as our savior. Words coming from Gabriel's mouth announce to Mary that she is the chosen mother of Christ. Van Eyck painted Mary's response upside down as though her words are being "read" from heaven above.

Gabriel carries the lily of Mary's chastity. The pitcher, basin, and towel seen beyond Mary prefigure Pilate washing his hands of Christ's innocent blood at his trial. Above the basin is a trefoil window, symbolizing the Holy Trinity. The other window represents the awakening of Mary to her destiny as mother of Christ.

CHRIST WILL BE CONCEIVED BY A VIRGIN

OLD TESTAMENT PROPHECY

Therefore the Lord himself will give you a sign: The virgin will be with child and will give birth to a son, and will call him Immanuel. — ISAIAH 7:14, C 735 BC

NEW TESTAMENT FULFILLMENT

This is how the birth of Jesus Christ came about: His mother Mary was pledged to be married to Joseph, but before they came together, she was found to be with child through the Holy Spirit. . . an angel of the Lord appeared to him (Joseph) in a dream and said, "Joseph, son of David, do not be afraid to take Mary home as your wife, because what is conceived in her is from the Holy Spirit. She will give birth to a son, and you are to give him the name Jesus, because he will save his people from their sins."

All this took place to fulfill what the Lord had said through the prophet: "The virgin will be with child and will give birth to a son, and they will call him Immanuel" —which means, "God with us." — MATTHEW 1:18, 20-23, C 6-2 BC

LEONARDO DA VINCI (1452-1519)

The Virgin of the Rocks, 1482

Louvre, Paris, France. Scala/Art Resource, NY

Leonardo da Vinci gives us a striking natural setting as a background for the Madonna. Her arm is shielding John the Baptist. As the angel to the right of Mary points to John, the infant Christ raises his hand in blessing, foreshadowing his birthright.

Much has been made of the enigmatic environment Leonardo used as a backdrop for this scene. The dark grotto with the mysterious light emerging in the background, has been interpreted sometimes as Leonardo's vision of the place where "life"—here in the sense of spiritual or eternal life—begins, brought about by Christ. Hence the lush, beautifully rendered vegetation emerging from the darkness.

OLD TESTAMENT PROPHECIES

The Lord had said to Abram, "Leave your country, your people and your father's household and go to the land I will show you. I will make you into a great nation and I will bless you; I will make your name great, and you will be a blessing. I will bless those who bless you, and whoever curses you I will curse; and all peoples on earth will be blessed through you."
— GENESIS 12:1-3, C 1921 BC

God said to him, "Your name is Jacob, but you will no longer be called Jacob; your name will be Israel." So he named him Israel. And God said to him, "I am God Almighty; be fruitful and increase in number. A nation and a community of nations will come from you, and kings will come from your body. The land I gave to Abraham and Isaac I also give to you, and I will give this land to your descendants after you." — GENESIS 35:10-12, C 1732 BC

NEW TESTAMENT FULFILLMENT

. . . the people of Israel. Theirs is the adoption as sons; theirs the divine glory, the covenants, the receiving of the law, the temple worship and the promises. Theirs are the patriarchs, and from them is traced the human ancestry of Christ, who is God over all, forever praised! Amen.
— ROMANS 9:4-5, C AD 58

MARC CHAGALL (1887-1985)

The Yellow Crucifixion, 1943

©2000 ARS, NY. Musee National d'Art Moderne, Centre Georges Pompidou, Paris, France, Art Resource, NY

In this painting, Jewish artist Marc Chagall paints Jesus as an observant Jew wearing phylacteries on his head and prayer straps on his arm. These ceremonial items were inscribed with portions from the Hebrew Scriptures. The scroll of the Torah appears on the left side of the painting. Under that we see Jacob's ladder. The lower portion shows persecuted Russian Jews from the artist's hometown of Vitebsk, Russia.

THE MESSIAH WILL BE BORN IN BETHLEHEM

OLD TESTAMENT PROPHECY

But you, Bethlehem Ephrathah, though you are small among the clans of Judah, out of you will come for me one who will be ruler over Israel, whose origins are from of old, from ancient times.
— MICAH 5:2, C 700 BC

NEW TESTAMENT FULFILLMENT

When King Herod heard this he was disturbed, and all Jerusalem with him. When he had called together all the people's chief priests and teachers of the law, he asked them where the Christ was to be born. "In Bethlehem in Judea," they replied, "for this is what the prophet has written."
— MATTHEW 2: 3-5, C 6-2 BC

Even when King Herod wanted to know where the Messiah, Christ would be born, the chief priests didn't have to consult; they knew. It was known by everyone who studied Tenach, the Old Testament, that the Messiah would be born in Bethlehem.

The word "Beth" means house; "Lechem" means bread. Bethlehem — the House of Bread. Out of Bethlehem came the Bread of Life!

SANDRO BOTTICELLI (1444-1510)

The Adoration of the Magi, 1475-1476

Uffizi, Florence, Italy. Scala/Art Resource, NY

The crumbled ruins represent the future crumbling of Jerusalem and its temple. Yet in these ruins we see new life. Small trees have begun to grow between the stones.

Perched on the upper right wall of this crumbling building we see the peacock of immortality, foreshadowing Christ's resurrection. The Magi remove their crowns as a sign of submission to the One greater than they.

CHRIST WILL DESCEND FROM ABRAHAM, ISAAC, AND JACOB

ABRAHAM

OLD TESTAMENT PROPHECY

The angel of the Lord called to Abraham from heaven a second time and said, ". . . through your seed all nations on earth will be blessed, because you have obeyed me."
— GENESIS 22:15,18, C 1872 BC

NEW TESTAMENT FULFILLMENT

A record of the genealogy of Jesus Christ the son of David, the son of Abraham.
— MATTHEW 1:1, C 6-2 BC

The prophecy about Abraham's seed recorded in Genesis is thoroughly explained in Galatians:

The promises were spoken to Abraham and to his seed. The Scripture does not say "and to seeds," meaning many people, but "and to your seed," meaning one person, who is Christ. —
GALATIANS 3:16, C AD 49 OR AD 55

Abraham and the Three Angels
Psalter of Ingeburg of Denmark, ms.9/1695, f.10v, c.1210
Musee Conde, Chantilly, France. Giraudon/Art Resource, NY

This illuminated manuscript page relates the story of Abraham's visit by three angels. As stated in Genesis 18:1-10, one of these angels was God—the Lord presenting himself in the form of a man. Once he realized that the visitors were angels, Abraham washed their feet and fed them. After eating, the angels told Abraham that his wife, Sarah, would bear a son. Sarah overheard this and began laughing. She was beyond her eightieth year and clearly unable to bear children. However, shortly after that, she conceived and gave birth to Isaac. The name Isaac is Hebrew for "laughter."

1

Si come abraham uit trois angeles 7 un en aora.

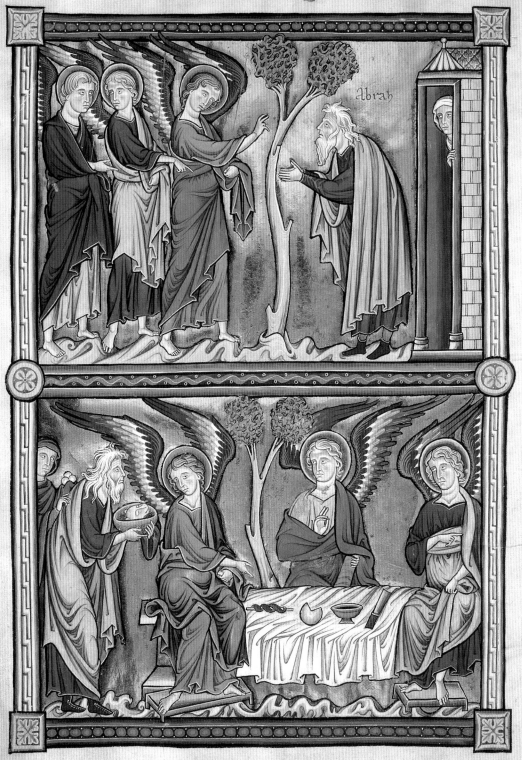

Si come il leur dona a maingier.

Isaac

....

Old Testament Prophecy

But God said to him (Abraham), "Do not be so distressed about the boy and your maidservant. Listen to whatever Sarah tells you, because it is through Isaac that your offspring will be reckoned." — GENESIS 21:12, C 1892 BC

New Testament Fulfillment

Now Jesus himself. . . was about thirty years old when he began his ministry. he was the son. . . of Isaac, the son of Abraham. . . — LUKE 3:23,34, C AD 26

FILIPPO BRUNELLESCHI (1377-1446)

Sacrifice of Isaac, 1401-1402

Competition panel. Museo Nazionale del Bargello, Florence, Italy. Scala/Art Resource, NY

God asked Abraham to take his son to the hilltop and sacrifice him. Abraham did as he was told. He instructed Isaac to carry the wood for the sacrificial pyre. Once they reached the mount, Isaac was tied down and Abraham grabbed his dagger. But just as Abraham drew his knife into the air, an angel swooped down from heaven and clutched Abraham's arm, sparing Isaac's life within a second. The angel told Abraham, "Now I know that you fear God, because you have not withheld from me your son, your only son." (Genesis 22:12)

Brunelleschi masterfully brings us the anxiety of this moment. Note the fiercely drawn knife, Abraham's garments flailing in the wind, the rigid tension of Isaac's muscles, and finally, the angel diving down to seize Abraham's arm.

Here are two compelling parallels of Isaac to Christ. Abraham offering his son is a powerful foreshadowing of God's sacrifice of his own son, and Isaac carrying the wood for his own death pyre prefigures Christ carrying his own cross to Golgotha.

JACOB

OLD TESTAMENT PROPHECY

I see him, but not now; I behold him, but not near. A star will come out of Jacob; a scepter will rise out of Israel. . . — **NUMBERS 24:17, C 1410 BC**

NEW TESTAMENT FULFILLMENT

Now Jesus himself . . . was about thirty years old when he began his ministry. He was the son . . . of Jacob, the son of Isaac . . . — **LUKE 3:23,34. C AD 26**

And he will reign over the house of Jacob forever; his kingdom will never end.
— **LUKE 1:33, C 6-2 BC**

JUSEPE DE RIBERA (LO SPAGNOLETTO) (C. 1590-1652)

Isaac Blessing Jacob, 1637

Prado, Madrid, Spain/Bridgeman Art Library

The blessing of Jacob is a common theme in the Renaissance period. In this narrative, Isaac is old, blind and near death. The time has come to pass his legacy to one of his sons, Esau or Jacob. Isaac intended Esau to receive his blessing. As we see in this image, Jacob has goatskin wrapped around his arm. Esau was a very hairy man and Isaac would recognize Jacob's hairless arms. In order to compel Isaac to mistake one brother for the other, Rebecca covered Jacob with goatskin. Jacob was chosen by God over Esau. And so, Jacob did indeed receive Isaac's blessing.

BOAZ AND RUTH

OLD TESTAMENT PROPHECY

Through the offspring the Lord gives you by this young woman, may your family be like that of Perez, whom Tamar bore to Judah. So Boaz took Ruth and she became his wife. Then he went to her, and the Lord enabled her to conceive, and she gave birth to a son. The women said to Naomi: "Praise be to the Lord, who this day has not left you without a kinsman-redeemer. May he become famous throughout Israel! He will renew your life and sustain you in your old age. . . . And they named him Obed. He was the father of Jesse, the father of David. — RUTH 4:12-17, C 1100 BC

NEW TESTAMENT FULFILLMENT

Now Jesus himself was about thirty years old when he began his ministry. He was the son . . . of David, the son of Jesse, the son of Obed, the son of Boaz . . . — LUKE 3:23, 32, C AD 26

Salmon the father of Boaz, whose mother was Rahab, Boaz the father of Obed, whose mother was Ruth, Obed the father of Jesse, and Jesse the father of King David. — MATTHEW 1:5, C AD 26

When he heard that it was Jesus of Nazareth, he began to shout, "Jesus, Son of David, have mercy on me!" Many rebuked him and told him to be quiet, but he shouted all the more, "Son of David, have mercy on me!"— MARK 10:47-48, C AD 29

NICOLAS POUSSIN (1594-1665)

The Summer or Ruth and Boaz, 1660-1664

Louvre, Paris,France. Giraudon/Art Resource, NY

After Naomi's husband and sons died, Ruth, her daughter-in-law, refused to leave her. Naomi urged Ruth return to her own family, to try to find another husband, continue her life. But Ruth vowed to spend the rest of her days in Naomi's company. After traveling to Bethlehem they found work in a wheat field owned by Boaz. When Boaz heard of the great deed Ruth had done, forsaking her life for the welfare of her mother-in-law, he praised her highly. Poussin has brought us that touching moment: "At this, she bowed down with her face to the ground. She exclaimed, 'Why have I found such favor in your eyes that you notice me—a foreigner?' " (Ruth 2:10)

29

JESSE

OLD TESTAMENT PROPHECIES

A shoot will come up from the stump of Jesse; from his roots a branch will bear fruit. — ISAIAH 11:1, C 734 BC

In that day the Root of Jesse will stand as a banner for the peoples; the nations will rally to him, and his place of rest will be glorious. — ISAIAH 11:10, C 734 BC

NEW TESTAMENT FULFILLMENT

Now Jesus himself. . . was about thirty years old when he began his ministry. He was the son. . . of Jesse. . . the son of Jacob. . . — LUKE 3:23,31,34, C AD 26

The Tree of Jesse (Christ's Genealogy)
From Psalter of Ingeburg of Denmark, 13th century
Musee Conde, Chantilly, France. Giraudon/Art Resource, NY

The tree of Jesse has been illustrated numerous times, but perhaps never as richly as in this depiction. The full lineage of Christ is not shown, but those ancestors who are shown have been given utmost attention within this magnificent gold backdrop.

Reading the tree from bottom to top: Adam lies asleep as a shoot springs forth from his side. From that shoot rises Jesse, then David. The Virgin Mary and Christ are at the top.

Le arbre.

CHRIST WILL COME FROM THE HOUSE OF DAVID

OLD TESTAMENT PROPHECY

For to us a child is born, to us a son is given, and the government will be on his shoulders. And he will be called Wonderful Counselor, Mighty God, Everlasting Father, Prince of Peace. Of the increase of his government and peace there will be no end. He will reign on David's throne and over his kingdom, establishing and upholding it with justice and righteousness from that time on and forever. The zeal of the Lord Almighty will accomplish this. — ISAIAH 9:6-7, C 734 BC

The Lord swore an oath to David, a sure oath that he will not revoke: "One of your own descendants I will place on your throne. . . " — PSALMS 132:11

NEW TESTAMENT FULFILLMENT

A record of the genealogy of Jesus Christ the son of David, the son of Abraham. . . — MATTHEW 1:1, C AD 26

After removing Saul, he made David their king. He testified concerning him: "I have found David, son of Jesse a man after my own heart; he will do everything I want him to do. From this man's descendants God has brought to Israel the Savior Jesus, as he promised."
— ACTS 13:22-23, C AD 45

Friends and foes alike called Jesus "Thou son of David." This was not challenged. The temple was standing and anyone could check the official genealogical record which would not be destroyed until 70 A.D. Jesus' genealogy has been preserved in the new testament.

MICHELANGELO BUONARROTI (1475-1564)

David, 1501-1504

Accademia, Florence, Italy. Scala/Art Resource, NY

The future king holds a slingshot in his left hand and a rock in his right. He is prepared for his fierce battle against the mighty Goliath. The battle between David and Goliath is traditionally portrayed as David's victory after the battle. Here Michelangelo has portrayed the moment before battle. He looks toward the battle line totally relaxed; his muscles are not tensed. He has refused to wear the armor given to him by Saul. This is his moment of truth. He must make a decision to approach Goliath and fight or to run away, in much the same way that Christ made the decision to enter Jerusalem. The confident serenity David portrays alludes to his future victory as king.

God inspired the beautiful and hopeful prophecies of Isaiah who gave us several titles for the Messiah to come, such as, "Wonderful, Counselor, Mighty God, Everlasting Father, and Prince of Peace." (Isaiah 9:6) Less known are the artistic hints Isaiah gives us of the actual name of "Jesus" in his Old Testament book written about 734 B.C. The original Hebrew word for Jesus is "Yeshua," with variants like "Yasha" and "Yesha." All these are correctly translated "salvation." With this awareness we invite you to read, and hear, this majestic passage from Isaiah 12:1-6 substituting the actual Hebrew word "Yeshua" (Jesus) for our English word "salvation."

And in that day thou shalt say, O Lord, I will praise thee: though thou wast angry with me, thine anger is turned away, and thou comfortedst me. Behold God (is) my yeshua; I will trust, and not be afraid: for the Lord Jehovah (is) my strength and (my) song; he also is become my yeshua. Therefore with joy shall ye draw water out of the wells of yeshua. And in that day shall ye say, Praise the Lord, call upon his name, declare his doings among the people, make mention that his name is exalted. Sing unto the Lord; for he hath done excellent things: this (is) known in all the earth. Cry out and shout, thou inhabitant of Zion: for great (is) the Holy One if Israel in the midst of thee. — ISAIAH 12:1-6, C 740-680 BC

Isaiah does even more with the variant "Yesha" in 62:11:

Jehovah has made proclamation to the ends of the earth; say to the daughter of Zion, "See your yesha comes. Behold his reward is with him."— ISAIAH 62:11, C 740-680 BC

Here, salvation is a person, and a male person at that in spite of the fact that yesha and/or yasha are feminine words.

In the book of Revelation, Jesus predicts his second coming with the words:

"Behold, I am coming soon! My reward is with me."— REVELATION 22:12, C AD 90

He is also called by another name given to us in Isaiah:

"Therefore the Lord himself will give you a sign: The virgin will be with child and will give birth to a son, and they will call him Immanuel."— ISAIAH 7:14, C 740-680 BC

The name we use the most was sent from the very Throne of God:

She will give birth to a son, and you are to give him the name Jesus (yeshua), because he will save his people from their sins. All this took place to fulfill what the Lord had said through the prophet: "The virgin will be with child and will give birth to a son, and they will call him Immanuel"—which means, "God with us."— MATTHEW 1:21-23, C 6-2 BC

*Christ Pantocrator, below the Madonna Enthroned with Angels and Apostles
view of the mosaic cycle in the main apse, completed c. 1183 (photo)*

Duomo, Monreale, Sicily, Italy/Peter Willi/Bridgeman Art Library

This image portrays all-knowing, omnipotent Christ. In his left hand Christ holds a scroll perhaps bearing one of the many Old Testament prophecies foretelling his life. The Pantocrator is a vision of Christ's reign over all souls.

OLD TESTAMENT PROPHECY

For to us a child is born, to us a son is given, and the government will be on his shoulders. And he will be called Wonderful Counselor, Mighty God, Everlasting Father, Prince of Peace.

— ISAIAH 9:6, C 734 BC

NEW TESTAMENT FULFILLMENT

And there were shepherds living out in the fields nearby, keeping watch over their flocks at night. An angel of the Lord appeared to them, and the glory of the Lord shone around them, and they were terrified. But the angel said to them, "Do not be afraid. I bring you good news of great joy that will be for all the people. Today in the town of David a Savior has been born to you; he is Christ the Lord. This will be a sign to you: You will find a baby wrapped in cloths and lying in a manger." Suddenly a great company of the heavenly host appeared with the angels, praising God and saying, "Glory to God in the highest, and on earth peace to men, on whom his favor rests."

— LUKE 2:8-14, C 6-2 BC

HUGO VAN DER GOES (C.1420-82)

The Portinari Triptych, central panel, Adoration of the Shepherds, 1475-1476

Uffizi, Florence, Italy. Alinari/Art Resource, NY

Van der Goes fills this painting with symbolism alluding to Christ's lineage. The upper right hand corner of the painting positions the angels directly above the shepherds as they learn of the birth of Christ. In the background on one of the buildings is a harp—the symbol on the coat of arms of the House of David, of which Christ is a descendant. The artist contrasts the palace of David with the humble, ramshackle stable to emphasize Christ's origin as both regal and humble. The point is further stressed by the prominence of the shepherds who arrive first, ahead of the Magi (usually depicted in "Adoration" scenes). In Van der Goes' *Adoration,* Christ is the king of heaven but more importantly he is the redeemer of the humble and the ordinary. Other symbols abound: Joseph has taken off his shoes to show he is on holy ground, the flowers, vase, and glass symbolize the humility and sorrow of Mary as well as the virgin birth (like the glass which allows the sunlight to pass through, she is the vessel for Christ but remains pure).

OLD TESTAMENT PROPHECIES

The Lord rises upon you and his glory appears over you. Nations will come to your light, and kings to the brightness of your dawn. . . the wealth on the seas will be brought to you, to you the riches of the nations will come. Herds of camels will cover your land, young camels of Midian and Ephah. And all from Sheba will come, bearing gold and incense and proclaiming the praise of the Lord.

— ISAIAH 60:2-3, 5-6, C 1250 BC

The kings of Tarshish and of distant shores will bring tribute to him; the kings of Sheba and Seba will present him gifts. All kings will bow down to him and all nations will serve him.

— PSALM 72:10-11

NEW TESTAMENT FULFILLMENT

When they saw the star, they were overjoyed. On coming to the house, they saw the child with his mother Mary, and they bowed down and worshiped him. Then they opened their treasures and presented him with gifts of gold and of incense and of myrrh.

— MATTHEW 2:10-11, C AD 26

ALBRECHT DÜRER (1471-1528)

Adoration of the Magi, 1504

Uffizi, Florence, Italy. Scala/Art Resource, NY

Dürer's painting contains much of the same symbolism as Botticelli's *Adoration of the Magi*. The setting is the center of desolate remnants of a former community. Again, these remains foster new life abundantly popping up. Rather than the peacock, Dürer has chosen to use the beetle in the lower right hand corner as reference to Christ's immortality. For centuries the curious birthing ritual of the beetle has inspired its use as a symbol of the triumph of life over death. Dürer was particularly fond of this symbol as it appears repeatedly throughout his works. The Magi again remove their crowns in submission.

THE HOLY FAMILY WILL FLEE TO EGYPT
TO ESCAPE THE MASSACRE OF THE INNOCENTS

OLD TESTAMENT PROPHECY

This is what the Lord says: "A voice is heard in Ramah, mourning and great weeping, Rachel weeping for her children and refusing to be comforted, because her children are no more."
— JEREMIAH 31:15, C 596 BC

NEW TESTAMENT FULFILLMENT

When they had gone, an angel of the Lord appeared to Joseph in a dream. "Get up," he said, "take the child and his mother and escape to Egypt. Stay there until I tell you, for Herod is going to search for the child to kill him." So he got up, took the child and his mother during the night and left for Egypt, where he stayed until the death of Herod. And so was fulfilled what the Lord had said through the prophet: "Out of Egypt I called my son." When Herod realized that he had been outwitted by the Magi, he was furious, and he gave orders to kill all the boys in Bethlehem and its vicinity who were two years old and under, in accordance with the time he had learned from the Magi. Then what was said through the prophet Jeremiah was fulfilled: "A voice is heard in Ramah, weeping and great mourning, Rachel weeping for her children and refusing to be comforted, because they are no more." — MATTHEW 2:13-18, C 6-2 BC

GUIDO RENI (1575-1642)

Massacre of the Innocents, 1611

Pinacoteca Nazionale, Bologna, Italy. Scala/Art Resource, NY

The Massacre of the Innocents was a terrible atrocity which Reni portrays quite movingly. Mothers are frantically trying to save their children, as many babies lie dead upon the floor. Fleeing to the right of the frame we see Elizabeth, with John the Baptist hidden in her cloak. Next to Elizabeth, Rachel is kneeling on the ground "weeping . . . because her children are no more." In the clouds above, angels grasp bundles of palms, the symbol of the martyr.

OUT OF EGYPT I WILL CALL MY SON

OLD TESTAMENT PROPHECIES

When that day dawns, the king of Israel will be completely destroyed.

When Israel was a child, I loved him, and out of Egypt I called my son.
— HOSEA 10:15-11:1, C 725 BC

NEW TESTAMENT FULFILLMENT

After Herod died, an angel of the Lord appeared in a dream to Joseph in Egypt and said, "Get up, take the child and his mother and go to the land of Israel, for those who were trying to take the child's life are dead." So he got up, took the child and his mother and went to the land of Israel.
— MATTHEW 2:19-21, C 4 BC – AD 6

And so was fulfilled what the Lord had said through the prophet: "Out of Egypt I called my son." — MATTHEW 2:15, C 4 BC – AD 6

GIOTTO DI BONDONE (1266-1336)

The Flight into Egypt, 1306

Scrovegni Chapel, Padua, Italy. Cameraphoto/Art Resource, NY

Joseph guides the Holy Family across the picture plane as the angel of the Lord watches over. Giotto has created a harmonious rhythm by allowing the clothing of the participants to mimic the forms of the rocks. Note that in the background, wherever the Christ child has passed, unexpected trees spring forth in this desert; whereas, immediately ahead of them the land is barren.

15
THE MESSIAH WILL COME
BEFORE JUDAH LOSES ITS SOVEREIGN POWER

OLD TESTAMENT PROPHECY

You are a lion's cub, O Judah; you return from the prey, my son. Like a lion he crouches and lies down, like a lioness—who dares to rouse him? The scepter will not depart from Judah, nor the ruler's staff from between his feet, until he comes to whom it belongs and the obedience of the nations is his. — GENESIS 49:9-10, C 1689 BC

The Messiah had to come before Judah lost its scepter, or tribal identity. "Even though Judah, during seventy years of captivity at Babylon, had been deprived of national sovereignty, the people never lost their 'tribal staff,' their national identity; and they always had their own judges, even in captivity.
Twenty-two years before the Lord Jesus was crucified, the Sanhedrin lost the power of passing the death sentence when Judea became a Roman province. Rabbi Rachmon says, 'When the members of the Sanhedrin found themselves deprived of their right over life and death, a general consternation took possession of them; they covered their heads with ashes and their bodies with sackcloth exclaiming, "Woe unto us, for the scepter has departed from Judah and the Messiah has not come." ' The rabbis did not realize that the Messiah had come. From this it is apparent that they considered Genesis 49:10 Messianic, and had a clear concept of its meaning." — THE MESSIAH IN BOTH TESTAMENTS, BY FRED JOHN MELDAU

Pilate said "Take him yourselves and judge him by your own law." "But we have no right to execute anyone." The Jews objected. — JOHN 18:31, C AD 33

LOUIS FRANÇOIS CASSIS (1756-1827)

The Sepulchral Monument of the Kings of Judah,
plate 25 from Volume III of a 'Voyage Pittoresque', engraved by Tillard, 1799
Private Collection/The Stapleton Collection/Bridgeman Art Library

The sepulchre, like a mausoleum, served as a burial chamber for the wealthy. The massive structure illustrated here conveys more than the importance of the kings of Judah. It also testifies to the respect in which they were held by those who knew the Messiah would descend from them.

JOHN THE BAPTIST WILL PREPARE THE WAY FOR CHRIST

OLD TESTAMENT PROPHECY

A voice of one calling: "In the desert prepare the way for the Lord; make straight in the wilderness a highway for our God." — ISAIAH 40:3, C 690 BC

"See, I will send my messenger, who will prepare the way before me. Then suddenly the Lord you are seeking will come to his temple; the messenger of the covenant whom you desire, will come," says the Lord Almighty. — MALACHI 3:1, 430 BC

NEW TESTAMENT FULFILLMENT

And so John came, baptizing in the desert region and preaching a baptism of repentance for the forgiveness of sins. — MARK 1:4, C AD 26

"I baptize with water," John replied, "but among you stands one you do not know. He is the one who comes after me, the thongs of whose sandals I am not worthy to untie." — JOHN 1:26-27, C AD 26

John himself recognized his purpose in preparing the way for Christ.

DOMENICO VENEZIANO (1405?-1461)

Saint John in the Desert, c. 1445

Samuel H. Kress Collection, ©2000 Board of Trustees, National Gallery of Art, Washington.

This painting is a departure from the traditional depictions of John the Baptist. No longer does the lamb accompany him. Nor does he carry the cross staff. Rather, he sheds the clothes of a common man to don the camel hide of an ascetic, to begin his ministry to prepare the way for Jesus.

OLD TESTAMENT PROPHECY

The Spirit of the Lord will rest on him—the Spirit of wisdom and of understanding, the Spirit of counsel and of power, the Spirit of knowledge and of the fear of the Lord.
— ISAIAH 11:2, C 734 BC

NEW TESTAMENT FULFILLMENT

When all the people were being baptized Jesus was baptized too and as he was praying Heaven opened up and the Holy Spirit descended on him in bodily form like a dove. And a voice came from heaven: "You are my Son, whom I love; with you I am well pleased."— LUKE 3:21-22, C AD 26

Later, at the mountain where Jesus was transfigured. . .

While he was still speaking, a bright cloud enveloped them, and a voice from the cloud said, "This is my Son, whom I love; with him I am well pleased. Listen to Him!" When the disciples heard this, they fell face down to the ground, terrified. But Jesus came and touched them. "Get up," he said. "Don't be afraid." — MATTHEW 17:5-7, C AD 32

PIETRO PERUGINO (1448-1523)

The Baptism of Christ, c.1498

Kunsthistorisches Museum, Vienna, Austria. Erich Lessing/Art Resource, NY

The dove of the Holy Spirit descends upon this scene in blessing. John and Christ stand on opposite sides of the River Jordan. John baptizes Christ as others witness and wait for their baptism. Notice the array of vegetation behind Christ, whereas on John's side of the river the growth is sparse. This is signifying that John is merely a messenger of God, preparing the way for the Greater One. John holds the cross staff that both he and the lamb hold throughout art history.

OLD TESTAMENT PROPHECY

He humbled you, causing you to hunger and then feeding you with manna, which neither you nor your fathers had known, to teach you that man does not live on bread alone but on every word that comes from the mouth of the Lord. — DEUTERONOMY 8:3, C 1410 BC

NEW TESTAMENT FULFILLMENT

Then Jesus was led by the Spirit into the desert to be tempted by the devil. After fasting forty days and forty nights, he was hungry. The tempter came to him and said, "If you are the Son of God, tell these stones to become bread." Jesus answered, "It is written: 'Man does not live on bread alone, but on every word that comes from the mouth of God.'" — MATTHEW 4:3-4, C AD 26

Satan knew Jesus was the Messiah, and that is why he had to tempt him. Christ did not fall into temptation, but defeated the attacks of Satan by relying on the powerful word of God.

Jesus could have used any of his powers to defeat Satan, yet he used the Holy Word of God. This same Word of God is available to us today.

Baptism and Temptation of Christ, Psalter of Ingeburg of Denmark, 1210

MS 9/1695. Musee Conde, Chantilly, France. Giraudon/Art Resource, NY

After Christ's baptism he retreated to the desert for forty days. During this time Satan came to him. Recognizing Christ as the Messiah, Satan had to tempt him.

This illuminated manuscript depicts Matthew 4:4-7, the first two temptations with which Satan attempted to ensnare Christ: "The tempter came to him and said, 'If you are the Son of God, tell these stones to become bread.' Jesus answered, 'It is written: *Man does not live on bread alone, but on every word that comes from the mouth of God.*'" Then the devil took him to the Holy City and had him stand on the highest point of the temple. 'If you are the Son of God,' he said, 'throw yourself down. For it is written: *He will command his angels concerning you, and they will lift you up in their hands, so that you will not strike your foot against a stone.*' Jesus answered him, 'It is also written: *Do not put the Lord your God to the test.*'"

OLD TESTAMENT PROPHECIES

The Lord has sworn and will not change his mind: "You are a priest forever, in the order of Melchizedek." — PSALMS 110:4

Then Melchizedek, king of Salem brought out bread and wine. He was priest of God Most High, and he blessed Abram, saying, "Blessed be Abram by God Most High, Creator of heaven and Earth. And blessed be God Most High, who delivered your enemies into your hand."
— GENESIS 14:18-20, C 1913 BC

NEW TESTAMENT FULFILLMENT

Where Jesus, who went before us, has entered on our behalf. He has become a high priest forever, in the order of Melchizedek. — HEBREWS 6:20, C AD 64

But because Jesus lives forever, he has a permanent priesthood. Therefore he is able to save completely those who came to God through him, because he always lives to intercede for them. Such a high priest meets our need — one who is holy, blameless, pure, set apart from sinners, exalted, above the heavens. — HEBREWS 7:24-26, C AD 64

DIERIC BOUTS (C.1415-1475)

Abraham and Melchizedek (top) from the Altar of the Last Supper (left wing) wood, 1464-1468
Collegiale St. Pierre, Louvain, Belgium. Erich Lessing/Art Resource, NY

Abraham returns home from a victorious battle fought to rescue Lot; along the way he encounters Melchizedek. In Dieric Bouts' portrayal of this meeting Abraham begins to kneel in reverence to Melchizedek, who has suddenly appeared with bread and the golden chalice of wine, and who blesses Abraham.

20

CHRIST'S MINISTRY WILL
BEGIN IN GALILEE

OLD TESTAMENT PROPHECY

Nevertheless, there will be no more gloom for those who were in distress. In the past he humbled the land of Zebulun and the land of Naphtali, but in the future he will honor Galilee of the Gentiles, by the way of the sea, along the Jordan — ISAIAH 9:1, C 734 BC

NEW TESTAMENT FULFILLMENT

When Jesus heard that John had been put in prison, he returned to Galilee. Leaving Nazareth, he went and lived in Capernaum, which was by the lake in the area of Zebulun and Naphtali—to fulfill what was said through the prophet Isaiah: From that time on Jesus began to preach.

— MATTHEW 4:12,13,17, C AD 26

JACOPO TINTORETTO

(1518-1594)

Christ at the Sea of Galilee, c. 1575/1580

Samuel H. Kress Collection, ©2000 Board of Trustees, National Gallery of Art, Washington

Here at the Sea of Galilee, Christ saves his disciples from the storm. The boat protected by Christ becomes the symbol of the Church preserved through the stormy sea of human history. The mast and sail become a symbol of the cross. Also note the trees of life surrounding Christ and the new vegetation growing at his feet.

21

CHRIST WILL TEACH IN PARABLES

OLD TESTAMENT PROPHECY

I will open my mouth in parables; I will utter hidden things, things from of old. — PSALMS 78:2

NEW TESTAMENT FULFILLMENT

Jesus spoke all these things to the crowd in parables; he did not say anything to them without using a parable.
— MATTHEW 13:34, C AD 31

Jesus spoke in parables as a way to reach many.

The Mustard Seed

He told them another parable: "The kingdom of heaven is like a mustard seed, which a man took and planted in his field. Though it is the smallest of all your seeds, yet when it grows, it is the largest of garden plants and becomes a tree, so that the birds of the air come and perch in its branches."
— MATTHEW 13:31-32, C AD 31

The Unmerciful Servant

Therefore, the kingdom of heaven is like a king who wanted to settle accounts with his servants. As he began the settlement, a man who owed him ten thousand talents was brought to him. Since he was not able to pay, the master ordered that he and his wife and his children and all that he had be sold to repay the debt. The servant fell on his knees before him. "Be patient with me," he begged, "and I will pay back everything." The servant's master took pity on him, canceled the debt and let him go. But when that servant went out, he found one of his fellow servants who owed him a hundred denarii. He grabbed him and began to choke him. "Pay back what you owe me!" he demanded.

His fellow servant fell to his knees and begged him, "Be patient with me, and I will pay you back." But he refused. Instead, he went off and had the man thrown into prison until he could pay the debt. When the other servants saw what had happened, they were greatly distressed and went and told their master everything that had happened. Then the master called the servant in. "You wicked servant," he said, "I canceled all that debt of yours because you begged me to. Shouldn't you have had mercy on your fellow servant just as I had on you?" In anger his master turned him over to the jailers to be tortured, until he should pay back all he owed. This is how my heavenly Father will treat each of you unless you forgive your brother from your heart. — MATTHEW 18:23-35, C AD 32

JAN SANDERS VAN HEMESSEN (ACTIVE 1519-1555)

The Parable of the Unmerciful Servant, c. 1548-1552

Oil on panel, H. 81.6 cm; W.155.2 cm; University of Michigan Museum of Art, 1959/1.108

22

CHRIST WILL PROVE HIMSELF WITH MIRACLES

OLD TESTAMENT PROPHECY

T hen will the eyes of the blind be opened and the ears of the deaf unstopped. Then will the lame leap like a deer, and the mute tongue shout for joy. Water will gush forth in the wilderness and streams in the desert. — ISAIAH 35:5,6, C 740-680 BC

NEW TESTAMENT FULFILLMENT

J esus went through all the towns and villages, teaching in their synagogues, preaching the good news of the kingdom and healing every disease and sickness. — MATTHEW 9:35, C AD 31

Jesus replied, "Go back and report to John what you hear and see: The blind receive sight, the lame walk, those who have leprosy are cured, the deaf hear, the dead are raised, and the good news is preached to the poor. Blessed is the man who does not fall away on account of me."
— MATTHEW 11:4-6, C AD 31

When Jesus came into Peter's house, he saw Peter's mother-in-law lying in bed with a fever. he touched her hand and the fever left her, and she got up and began to wait on him. When evening came, many who were demon-possessed were brought to him, and he drove out the spirits with a word and healed all the sick. This was to fulfill what was spoken through the prophet Isaiah: "He took up our infirmities and carried our diseases." — MATTHEW 8:14-17, C AD 31

NICOLAS POUSSIN (1594-1665)

Detail of Jesus Healing the Blind of Jericho, 1650

Oil on canvas, 119 X 176 cm. Louvre, Paris, France. Erich Lessing/Art Resource, NY

As Christ is returning from the house of Jairus, two blind men approach and ask for his healing. Christ asks if they believe he is capable of such a miracle. Poussin has depicted the moment when they kneel down and reply in the affirmative. As recorded in Matthew 9:29-30, "Then he touched their eyes and said, 'According to your faith will it be done to you'; and their sight was restored." Christ places his hand over the eyes of a blind man and heals him as others look on in amazement.

The Spirit of the Sovereign Lord is on me, because the Lord has anointed me… to comfort all who mourn, and provide for those who grieve in Zion—to bestow on them a crown of beauty instead of ashes, the oil of gladness instead of mourning, and a garment of praise instead of a spirit of despair.
— ISAIAH 61:1-3, C 740-680 BC

"Lord," Martha said to Jesus, "if you had been here, my brother would not have died. But I know that even now God will give you whatever you ask." Jesus said to her, "Your brother will rise again." Martha answered, "I know he will rise again in the resurrection at the last day." Jesus said to her, "I am the resurrection and the life. He who believes in me will live, even though he dies; and whoever lives and believes in me will never die. Do you believe this?" "Yes, Lord," she told him, "I believe that you are the Christ, the Son of God, who was to come into the world." — JOHN 11:21-27, C AD 28-30

So they took away the stone. Then Jesus looked up and said, "Father, I thank you that you have heard me. I knew that you always hear me, but I said this for the benefit of the people standing here, that they may believe that you sent me." When he had said this, Jesus called in a loud voice, "Lazarus, come out!" The dead man came out, his hands and feet wrapped with strips of linen, and a cloth around his face. Jesus said to them, "Take off the grave clothes and let him go."
— JOHN 11:41-44, C AD 28-30

FRA ANGELICO (GUIDO DI PIETRO) (C. 1387-1455)

Resurrection of Lazarus, c. 1450

Armadio degli Argenti. Museo di San Marco, Florence, Italy. Scala/Art Resource/NY

Kneeling in front of Christ are Mary and Martha, sisters of Lazarus, while others reel back from the odor of death. They have been mourning his death for four days. Yet when Jesus questions Martha's faith, she does not hesitate to proclaim her belief. "Yes, Lord," she tells him, "I believe that you are the Christ, the Son of God, who was to come into the world." (John 11:27) Then he gives the order to remove the stone in front of Lazarus' burial cave and calls Lazarus' name. The man once dead walks again. From the rocky terrain of the tomb new trees spring to life.

DVCAM VOS DESEPVLCRIS POPVLVS MEVS. EÇECHIEL. XXXVII. C.

CLAMAVIT YHS VOCE MAG LAÇERE VENI FORAS. 7 STATIM PRODIIT Q ERAT MORTVVS. IO. II. C.

LAVAMINI MVNDI ESTOE AVFERE MALVM COGITATIONVM VESTRARVM. YSAI E. I. C.

See I will send you the prophet Elijah before that great and dreadful day of the Lord comes. He will turn the hearts of the fathers to their children and the hearts of the children to their fathers or else I will come and strike the land with a curse. — MALACHI 4:5-6, C 450-400 BC

Jesus confirms John the Baptist is Elijah:

"Why then do the teachers of the law say that Elijah must come first." Jesus replied, "To be sure, Elijah comes and will restore all things. But I tell you, Elijah has already come, and they did not recognize him, but have done to him everything they wished. In the same way the Son of Man is going to suffer at their hands. Then the disciples understood that he was talking to them about John the Baptist. — MATTHEW 17:10-13, C AD 28-30

St. John the Forerunner, Russian icon from the Deesis of the Church of St. Vlasius,
Novgorod School, 15th century (tempera on panel)
Museum of Art, Novgorod, Russia/Bridgeman Art Library

The Russian artist of this icon has portrayed the gentle man who came to prepare the way for Christ. His outstretched arms are a gesture of comfort as "he turn[s] the hearts of fathers to their children and the hearts of the children to their fathers."

63

OLD TESTAMENT PROPHECY

Moses said:

The Lord your God will raise up for you a prophet like me from among your own brothers. You must listen to him. . . The Lord said to me: "I will raise up for them a prophet like you from among their brothers; I will put my words in his mouth, and he will tell them everything I command him." — DEUTERONOMY 18:15,17,18, C 1410 BC

NEW TESTAMENT FULFILLMENT

For Moses said, "The Lord your God will raise up for you a prophet like me from among your own people; you must listen to everything he tells you. Anyone who does not listen to him will be completely cut off from among his people. Indeed, all the prophets from Samuel on, as many as have spoken, have foretold these days. And you are heirs of the prophets and of the covenant God made with your fathers. He said to Abraham, 'Through your offspring all peoples on earth will be blessed'." — ACTS 3:22-25, C AD 33

Not until halfway through the Feast did Jesus go up to the temple courts and begin to teach. The Jews were amazed and asked, "How did this man get such learning without having studied?" Jesus answered, "My teaching is not my own. It comes from him who sent me. If anyone chooses to do God's will, he will find out whether my teaching comes from God or whether I speak on my own." . . . On hearing his words, some of the people said, "Surely this man is the Prophet." — JOHN 7:14-17, 40, C AD 29

MICHELANGELO BUONARROTI (1475-1564)

Moses, from the Tomb of Julius II, 1513-1515

S. Pietro in Vincoli, Rome, Italy. Scala/Art Resource, NY

Michelangelo's powerful image of Moses shows the artist's deep understanding of the structure of the human body. Moses' tensed muscles suggest the fear he must have instilled in his followers after throwing down the stone tablets of the law. However, this image is not about the fearful, angry Moses. Here a seated Moses cradles the holy tablets. His garments are so lifelike they appear almost to be draped fabric rather than carved stone.

The lives of Moses and Christ had numerous parallels. Both were prophets. Just as Christ had to flee to Egypt to escape death as an infant, Exodus 2:1-10 describes how Moses escaped death as an infant. Moses' mother set Moses adrift in the river to evade the Pharaoh who ordered the wholesale slaughter of all male Israeli children. Exodus 12 recounts the instructions God gave to Moses to prepare the Israelis for exodus from Egypt. Part of the preparation included choosing a year-old male lamb without defect to roast and eat. The prescribed Passover meal was observed by Jesus and his disciples at the Last Supper.

After their flight from Egypt, many became hungry and feared death through starvation. God speaking to Moses miraculously provided manna to eat each day. (Exodus 16). This feeding of the multitudes foreshadowed Christ's miracle of feeding five thousand with a few loaves of bread and two fish.

Jesus desired to pay his taxes. To obtain money for his taxes and those of Peter, Jesus performs an amazing miracle. Peter was to take the first fish caught. That fish would have a coin in its mouth of the exact amount needed for the taxes.

J esus said to him. "But so that we may not offend them, go to the lake and throw out your line. Take the first fish you catch; open its mouth and you will find a four-drachma coin. Take it and give it to them for my tax and yours."

— MATTHEW 17:27, C AD 32

Give everyone what you owe him: If you owe taxes, pay taxes; if revenue, then revenue; if respect, then respect; if honor, then honor. —
ROMANS 13:7, C AD 60

MASACCIO (1401-1428)

The Tribute Money, 1427

S. Maria del Carmine, Florence, Italy. Scala/Art Resource, NY

Masaccio presents a narrative in three scenes. The significant scene is placed in the center. The apostles encircle Christ, discussing the payment of the tax. The tax collector stands in the foreground with his back to us. Christ tells Peter he will find the coin to pay the tax in the mouth of a fish. Masaccio uses artistic license to

foreshadow Peter's betrayal of Christ. As Christ points to the Sea of Galilee, Peter's expression is one of unwillingness and disbelief. He holds his left hand up as a distancing gesture of doubt. His frown of disapproval is mimicked by his uplifted eyebrow.

In the scene on the left, Peter has removed his robe and bends over to catch the fish. He extracts the coin from its mouth. Peter hands the coin to the tax collector on the right. Notice that in this scene as well as the first, the bodies of Peter and the tax collector are mirror images of each other, again showing Peter's future dual-persona.

OLD TESTAMENT PROPHECY

For zeal for your house consumes me, and the insults of those who insult you fall on me. — **PSALMS 69:9**

NEW TESTAMENT FULFILLMENT

So he made a whip out of cords, and drove all from the temple area, both sheep and cattle; he scattered the coins of the moneychangers and overturned their tables. To those who sold doves he said, "Get these out of here! How dare you turn my Father's house into a market!" His disciples remembered that it is written: "Zeal for your house will consume me." — **JOHN 2:15-17, C AD 30**

EL GRECO (DOMENICO THEOTOCOPULI)

(1541-1614)

Christ Driving the Traders from the Temple, c. 1600 (oil on canvas)

National Gallery, London, UK/Bridgeman Art Library

Vendors had taken over the temple. God's sanctuary was being turned into a marketplace. Angry over the utter disrespect, Christ wanted the temple cleansed.

In the upper left corner we see a painting of Adam and Eve and their Expulsion from the Garden of Eden. Likewise Christ is expelling the sinning vendors from God's house.

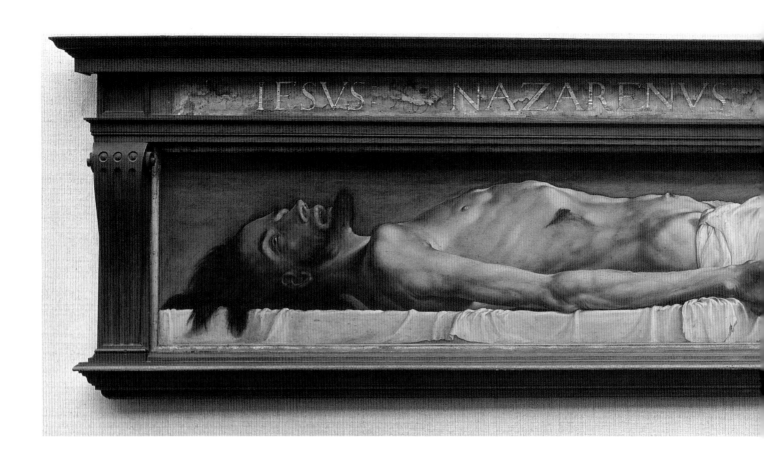

27
THE MESSIAH PREDICTS HIS OWN DEATH,
PERIOD OF ENTOMBMENT AND RESURRECTION

Christ knew what would happen to him once he entered Jerusalem.

Jesus took the Twelve aside and told them, "We are going up to Jerusalem, and everything that is written by the prophets about the Son of Man will be fulfilled. He will be handed over to the Gentiles. They will mock him, insult him, spit on him, flog him and kill him. On the third day he will rise again." The disciples did not understand any of this. Its meaning was hidden from them, and they did not know what he was talking about. — LUKE 18:31-34, C AD 33

From that time on Jesus began to explain to his disciples that he must go to Jerusalem and suffer many things at the hands of the elders, chief priests and teachers of the law, and that he must be killed and on the third day be raised to life. — MATTHEW 16:21, C AD 33

Now as Jesus was going up to Jerusalem, he took the twelve disciples aside and said to them, "We are going up to Jerusalem, and the Son of Man will be betrayed to the chief priests and the teachers of the law. They will condemn him to death and will turn him over to the Gentiles to be mocked and flogged and crucified. On the third day he will be raised to life!" — MATTHEW 20:17-19, C AD 33

Christ even the knew the horrible death he would endure as he was crucified on the cross.

"But I, when I am lifted up from the earth, will draw all men to myself." he said this to show the kind of death he was going to die. — JOHN 12:32-33, C AD 33

Christ did not have to die; he knew his fate and could have turned back anytime. He did not have to enter Jerusalem, but he did so of his own free will, knowing that in Jerusalem he would be betrayed, assaulted, and killed by one of history's most brutal methods. Jesus offered himself as a sacrifice for our sins, fulfilling prophecy.

HANS HOLBEIN THE YOUNGER (1497?-1543)

Dead Christ, 1521

Kunstmuseum, Basel, Switzerland. Giraudon/Art Resource, NY

Christ foresaw this exact scene of his lifeless body in the tomb. The gaping wound of his pierced side, his thin frail body, his pierced hands and feet. Holbein shows a tortured body. Yet his eyes are open to show he will rise. The inscription across the top of the tomb is the same inscription placed over Christ's head at his crucifixion: "Iesus Navarenus Rex Iudaeorum," Latin for "Jesus of Nazareth, King of the Jews."

JESUS FORETELLS WHERE A COLT MAY BE FOUND
FOR HIM TO RIDE INTO JERUSALEM

Jesus told his disciples where the colt was and that the owners would freely release the animal. The colt was unbroken yet followed the disciples and allowed Christ to ride him, showing no stubbornness or displeasure.

As they approached Jerusalem and came to Bethphage and Bethany at the Mount of Olives, Jesus sent two of his disciples, saying to them, "Go to the village ahead of you, and just as you enter it, you will find a colt tied there, which no one has ever ridden. Untie it and bring it here. If anyone asks you, 'Why are you doing this?' tell him, 'The Lord needs it and will send it back here shortly.' " They went and found a colt outside in the street, tied at a doorway. As they untied it, some people standing there asked, "What are you doing, untying that colt?" They answered as Jesus had told them to, and the people let them go. — MARK 11:1-6, C AD 33

DUCCIO DI BUONINSEGNA (C. 1260-1318)

Detail of Entry into Jerusalem (from the Maesta), 1308-1312

Museo dell'Opera Metropolitana, Siena, Italy. Scala/Art Resource, NY

In the lower right corner grows an olive tree of the Mount of Olives. Left of the tree is the doorway where the disciples found the colt that Christ prophesied. The river of life flows to the triumphal entry into Jerusalem.

OLD TESTAMENT PROPHECY

Rejoice greatly, O Daughter of Zion! Shout, Daughter of Jerusalem! See, your king comes to you, righteous and having salvation, gentle and riding on a donkey, on a colt, the foal of a donkey.
— ZECHARIAH 9:9, C 487 BC

NEW TESTAMENT FULFILLMENT

The disciples went and did as Jesus had instructed them. They brought the donkey and the colt, placed their cloaks on them, and Jesus sat on them. A very large crowd spread their cloaks on the road, while others cut branches from the trees and spread them on the road. The crowds that went ahead of him and those that followed shouted, "Hosanna to the Son of David! Blessed is he who comes in the name of the Lord! Hosanna in the highest!" When Jesus entered Jerusalem, the whole city was stirred and asked, "Who is this?" The crowds answered, "This is Jesus, the prophet from Nazareth in Galilee." — MATTHEW 21: 6-11, C AD 33

PIETRO LORENZETTI (1280-1348)

Entry of Christ into Jerusalem, 14th century

S. Francesco, Assisi, Italy. Scala/Art Resource, NY

As Christ enters Jerusalem he is greeted by a throng of people eager to hear his teachings. One man throws down his robe so that the colt carrying Christ may walk on it. This gesture is reserved for royalty. Some welcome Christ with palm branches, bringing the significance of Palm Sunday. In many entry scenes we see two figures climbing in trees. One is a child plucking more palms with which to shower Christ. The other is a nobleman from the city. He is too short to see over everyone, but no one moves out of his way so he must climb a tree to see the Savior enter. Christ's importance overshadows this man's regal status.

Then came the day of Unleavened Bread on which the Passover lamb had to be sacrificed. Jesus sent Peter and John, saying, "Go and make preparations for us to eat the Passover." "Where do you want us to prepare for it?" they asked. He replied, "As you enter the city, a man carrying a jar of water will meet you. Follow him to the house that he enters, and say to the owner of the house, 'The Teacher asks: Where is the guest room, where I may eat the Passover with my disciples?' He will show you a large upper room, all furnished. Make preparations there." They left and found things just as Jesus had told them. — LUKE 22:7-13, C AD 33

With thousands of people in town for Passover, every room in Jerusalem was occupied. How then did Jesus know where to find an empty place for the supper with his disciples? And how is it possible that there was room? Divine Intervention. Further, Jesus prophesied about a man carrying a jar of water—by no means a common sight. Men did not carry water from the well; only women did. Yet this day a man carried water just as Jesus had said, as a sign for Peter and John.

SALVADOR DALI (1904-1989)

The Sacrament of the Last Supper, 1955

Chester Dale Collection, ©2000 Board of Trustees, National Gallery of Art, Washington DC

In Salvador Dali's *Last Supper,* Christ gives his blessing while the disciples bow their heads in prayer. With his left hand he gestures toward himself. With his right he points upward to the image of his crucified body, portending his resurrection. Dali has taken a different approach with the Eucharistic offering. Rather than the golden chalice, the wine is contained in a clear glass, representing the purity of Christ's blood, body, and soul. Behind Christ three boats (signifying the Church) are afloat on the river of life.

JESUS PROPHESIES THE BETRAYAL OF JUDAS

OLD TESTAMENT PROPHECY

Even my close friend, whom I trusted, he who shared my bread, has lifted up his heel against me. —PSALM 41:9

NEW TESTAMENT PROPHECY AND FULFILLMENT

When evening came, Jesus arrived with the Twelve. While they were reclining at the table eating, he said, "I tell you the truth, one of you will betray me—one who is eating with me." They were saddened, and one by one they said to him, "Surely not I?" "It is one of the Twelve," he replied, "one who dips bread into the bowl with me." — MARK 14:17-20. C AD 33

Then Judas Iscariot, one of the Twelve, went to the chief priests to betray Jesus to them.

— MARK 14:10, C AD 33

LEONARDO DA VINCI (1452-1519)

The Last Supper, 1495-1497

S. Maria delle Grazie, Milan, Italy. Scala/Art Resource, NY

The Last Supper was a tempera experiment by Leonardo. Unfortunately, this experiment involved an unprimed surface and as a result the work began deteriorating even while da Vinci was alive.

This scene portrays the exact moment when Christ proclaimed, "One of you will betray me." Everyone is frantic that there could be a betrayer. Everyone, that is, except for Judas. Judas' face is the only one that is shadowed, signifying the dark nature of his betrayal. In a departure from tradition, Leonardo places Judas on the same side of the table as Christ, and by doing so allows us to see Judas clutching the bag containing the thirty pieces of silver. This same device reveals Peter grasping the knife he will later use to cut off the ear of Malchus.

Here Leonardo follows the growing Renaissance tradition of employing images of architecture in painting. A notable architectural detail is the window that frames Christ's head. The window has long been a symbol of revelation.

Peter replied, "Even if all fall away on account of you, I never will." "I tell you the truth," Jesus answered, "This very night, before the rooster crows, you will disown me three times." But Peter declared, "Even if I have to die with you, I will never disown you." And all of the other disciples said the same. — MATTHEW 26:33-35, C AD 33

Now Peter was sitting out in the courtyard, and a servant girl came to him. "You also were with Jesus of Galilee," she said. But he denied it before them all. "I don't know what you're talking about," he said. Then he went out to the gateway, where another girl saw him and said to the people there, "This fellow was with Jesus of Nazareth." He denied it again, with an oath: "I don't know the man!" After a little while, those standing there went up to Peter and said, "Surely you are one of them, for your accent gives you away." Then he began to call down curses on himself and he swore to them, "I don't know the man!" Immediately a rooster crowed. Then Peter remembered the word Jesus had spoken: "Before the rooster crows, you will disown me three times." And he went outside and wept bitterly.

— MATTHEW 26:69-75, C AD 33

DUCCIO DI BUONINSEGNA (C. 1260-1318)

The Flagellation of Christ, 1308-1311

Museo dell'Opera Metropolitana, Siena, Italy. Scala/Art Resource, NY

Christ is mocked and smitten as Pilate looks on. We see Peter departing into the gateway Matthew spoke of. Behind him is one of the women who questioned his knowledge of Jesus. We see from his frown, uplifted eyebrows, and raised hands (identical to the actions of Massaccio's Peter) that he is denying he knows Jesus. Directly above Peter, the cock begins to crow, fulfilling Christ's prophecy.

33
THROUGH JESUS EVERYTHING IS MADE NEW: THE PROMISE OF THE NEW COVENANT

OLD TESTAMENT PROPHECY

The time is coming," declares the Lord, "when I will make a new covenant with the house of Israel and with the house of Judah. It will not be like the covenant I made with your forefathers when I took them by the hand to lead them out of Egypt, because they broke my covenant, though I was a husband to them," declares the Lord.

— JEREMIAH 31:31-32, C 596 BC

NEW TESTAMENT FULFILLMENT

While they were eating, Jesus took bread, gave thanks and broke it, and gave it to his disciples, saying, "Take and eat; this is my body." Then he took the cup, gave thanks and offered it to them, saying, "Drink from it, all of you. This is my blood of the covenant, which is poured out for many for the forgiveness of sins." — MATTHEW 26: 26-28, C AD 33

COSIMO ROSSELLI (1439-1507)

Last Supper, 1482

Sistine Chapel, Vatican Palace, Vatican State. Scala/Art Resource, NY

As shown in Rosselli's *Last Supper,* Jesus the Son of God told his disciples that his death and resurrection sealed the new covenant with his people both Jew and Gentile. The old sacrifices were no longer needed. Jesus Christ became the ultimate and final sacrifice.

Cosimo Rosselli keeps with traditional placement of Judas on the opposite side of the table from Christ. Take note of the devil figure on Judas' back. This reflects Jesus' statement in John 6:70, "Have I not chosen you, the Twelve? Yet one of you is a devil!" In addition, Judas' halo is darkened where all other halos are a brilliant gold. On the floor we see several vessels containing the wine of the new covenant. Christ is speaking of what is to come while blessing this new covenant which promises redemption from sin.

Behind Christ are panels portraying the significant events which are to follow Christ's last meal. Reading from left to right, we see the Agony in the Garden, the Betrayal of Judas, and the Crucifixion.

Now there was a man of the Pharisees named Nicodemus, a member of the Jewish ruling council. He came to Jesus at night and said, "Rabbi, we know you are a teacher who has come from God. For no one could perform the miraculous signs you are doing if God were not with Him." In reply Jesus declared, "I tell you the truth, no one can see the kingdom of God unless he is born again." "How can a man be born when he is old?" Nicodemus asked. "Surely he cannot enter a second time into his mother's womb to be born!" Jesus answered, "I tell you the truth, no one can enter the kingdom of God unless he is born of water and the Spirit. Flesh gives birth to flesh, but the Spirit gives birth to Spirit. You should not be surprised at my saying, 'You must be born again.' The wind blows wherever it pleases. You hear its sound, but you cannot tell where it comes from or where it is going. So it is with everyone born of the Spirit." — JOHN 3:1-8, C AD 30

Later, Joseph of Arimathea asked Pilate for the body of Jesus. Now Joseph was a disciple of Jesus, but secretly, because he feared the Jews. With Pilate's permission, he came and took the body away. He was accompanied by Nicodemus, the man who earlier had visited Jesus at night. Nicodemus brought a mixture of myrrh and aloes, about seventy-five pounds. Taking Jesus' body, the two of them wrapped it, with the spices, in strips of linen. This was in accordance with Jewish burial customs. At the place where Jesus was crucified, there was a garden, and in the garden a new tomb in which no one had ever been laid. — JOHN 19:38-41, C AD 33

MICHAEL WOLGEMUT OR WOLGEMUTH (1434-1519)

St. Joseph and Nicodemus on gold ground panels (detail)

Christie's Images, London, UK/Bridgeman Art Library

Nicodemus and Joseph of Arimathea were present during the deposition and burial of Christ. Here we see Nicodemus accompanied with the pincers he used to remove the nails from Christ. Joseph, on the right, is holding the strips of linen used to wrap Christ's body. The linen was saturated with a mixture of costly spices and aloes, including myrrh, one of the first gifts Christ received at his birth.

THE PRICE OF THE BETRAYAL

Over five hundred years before it happened, God foretold the amount of money that Judas would be paid to betray Jesus.

OLD TESTAMENT PROPHECY

I told them, 'If you think it best, give me my pay; but if not, keep it.' So they paid me thirty pieces of silver. — ZECHARIAH 11:12, C 487 BC

NEW TESTAMENT FULFILLMENT

What are you willing to give me if I hand him over to you?" So they counted out for him thirty silver coins. — MATTHEW 26:15, C AD 33

BARNA DA SIENA, 14TH C.

The Elders Paying Judas

Collegiata, San Gimignano, Italy. Scala/Art Resource, NY

In this work, the chief priests are handing over to Judas the thirty pieces of silver. Each member of this scene wears a sinister look of uncommon evil.

OLD TESTAMENT PROPHECY

Even my close friend, whom I trusted, he who shared my bread, has lifted up his heel against me. — **PSALM 41:9**

NEW TESTAMENT FULFILLMENT

When evening came, Jesus was reclining at the table with the Twelve. And while they were eating, he said, "I tell you the truth, one of you will betray me." They were very sad and began to say to him one after the other, "Surely not I, Lord?" Jesus replied, "The one who has dipped his hand into the bowl with me will betray me. The Son of Man will go just as it is written about him. But woe to that man who betrays the Son of Man! It would be better for him if he had not been born." Then Judas, the one who would betray him, said, "Surely not I, Rabbi?" Jesus answered, "Yes, it is you." — **MATTHEW 26:20-25, C AD 33**

Now the betrayer had arranged a signal with them: "The one I kiss is the man; arrest him." Going at once to Jesus, Judas said, "Greetings, Rabbi!" and kissed him. Jesus replied, "Friend, do what you came for." Then the men stepped forward, seized Jesus and arrested him. With that, one of Jesus' companions reached for his sword, drew it out and struck the servant of the high priest, cutting off his ear. "Put your sword back in its place," Jesus said to him, "for all who draw the sword will die by the sword. Do you think I cannot call on my Father, and he will at once put at my disposal more than twelve legions of angels? But how then would the Scriptures be fulfilled that say it must happen in this way?" — **MATTHEW 26:48-54, C AD 33**

BARNA DA SIENA (14TH C.)

Kiss of Judas

Collegiata, San Gimignano, Italy, Scala/Art Resource, NY

Barna da Siena has rendered the moment of Judas' betrayal. Judas leans over to kiss Jesus, signaling to the soldiers the one they must arrest. Beneath Christ, Peter lunges toward Malchus to cut off his ear. As the soldiers close in to arrest Christ, the other disciples flee, just as prophesied by both Christ and Zechariah.

OLD TESTAMENT PROPHECY

And the Lord said to me, 'Throw it to the potter—the handsome price at which they priced me!' So I took the thirty pieces of silver and threw them into the house of the Lord to the potter.

— ZECHARIAH 11:13, C 487 BC

NEW TESTAMENT FULFILLMENT

When Judas, who had betrayed him, saw that Jesus was condemned, he was seized with remorse and returned the thirty silver coins to the chief priests and the elders. "I have sinned," he said, "for I have betrayed innocent blood." "What is that to us?" they replied. "That's your responsibility." So Judas threw the money into the temple and left. Then he went away and hanged himself. The chief priests picked up the coins and said, "It is against the law to put this into the treasury, since it is blood money." So they decided to use the money to buy the potter's field as a burial place for foreigners.

— MATTHEW 27:3-7, C AD 33

GIOTTO DI BONDONE (1266-1336)

Kiss of Judas, 1304-1306

Scrovegni Chapel, Padua Italy, Alinari/Art Resource, NY

The arresting procession has converged on Christ. Many are carrying torches symbolic of the Passion of Christ. One man is blowing a horn, signifying the resurrection. Again we see Peter's attack on Malchus. Christ's eyes are fixed firmly on the face of his betrayer. As Judas kisses Christ, his cloak almost fully envelopes him—as Judas' remorse will fully consume him before night's end.

OLD TESTAMENT PROPHECY

Awake, O sword, against my shepherd, against the man who is close to me!" declares the Lord Almighty. "Strike the shepherd, and the sheep will be scattered." — ZECHARIAH 13:7, C 487 BC

NEW TESTAMENT FULFILLMENT

Jesus told them, "This very night you will all fall away on account of me, for it is written: 'I will strike the shepherd, and the sheep of the flock will be scattered.'" — MATTHEW 26:31, C AD 33

Then everyone deserted him and fled. — MARK 14:50, C AD 33

MICHELANGELO BUONARROTI (1475-1564)

The Prophet Zaccariah, 1509

Sistine Chapel, Vatican Palace, Vatican State. Scala/Art Resource, NY

Michelangelo has characterized Zechariah as a gentle giant. He serenely sits, thumbing through the pages of his great works. Although he is covered in heavy robes, we can envision the brawn of his massive muscle structure. His body is capable of delivering a force as strong and powerful as his oracles of the Passion Week.

39

JESUS, A THREAT TO THE HIGH PRIEST, ADMITS TO BEING THE CHRIST, THE SON OF THE LIVING GOD

OLD TESTAMENT PROPHECY

The kings of the earth take their stand and the rulers of the earth gather together against the Lord and against his Anointed One. — PSALM 2:2

By oppression and judgment he was taken away. And who can speak of his descendants? For he was cut off from the land of the living for the transgression of my people. — ISAIAH 53:8, C 690 BC

NEW TESTAMENT FULFILLMENT

Therefore many of the Jews who had come to visit Mary, and had seen what Jesus did, put their faith in him. But some of them went to the Pharisees and told them what Jesus had done. Then the chief priests and the Pharisees called a meeting of the Sanhedrin.

"What are we accomplishing?" they asked. "Here is this man performing many miraculous signs. If we let him go on like this, everyone will believe in him, and then the Romans will come and take away both our place and our nation." Then one of them, named Caiaphas, who was high priest that year, spoke up, "You know nothing at all! You do not realize that it is better for you that one man die for the people than that the whole nation perish." He did not say this on his own, but as high priest that year he prophesied that Jesus would die for the Jewish nation, and not only for that nation but also for the scattered children of God, to bring them together and make them one. So from that day on they plotted to take his life. — JOHN 11:45-53, C AD 33

The high priest said to him "I charge you under oath by the living God: Tell us if you are the Christ the Son of God?" "Yes it is as you say," Jesus replied. "But I say to all of you in the future you will see the Son of Man sitting at the right hand of the Mighty One and coming on the clouds of heaven." Then the high priest tore his clothes and said, "He has spoken blasphemy. Why do we need any more witnesses? What do you think?" "He is worthy of death," they answered. Then they spit in his face and struck him with their fists. Others slapped him. . . — MATTHEW 26:63-67, C AD 33

GIOTTO DI BONDONE (1266-1336)

Christ before Caiaphas, 1304-1306

Scrovegni Chapel, Padua, Italy. Scala/Art Resource, NY

The tearing of one's own clothing has repeatedly been a sign of pronounced anguish in the Bible. Giotto portrays the moment when Jesus said, "I am the Christ, the Son of the Living God." Caiaphas rips his robe open as he orders Christ away to be beaten.

40

CHRIST WOULD NOT OPEN HIS MOUTH AT THE TRIAL

OLD TESTAMENT PROPHECY

He was oppressed and afflicted, yet he did not open his mouth; he was led like a lamb to the slaughter, and as a sheep before her shearers is silent, so he did not open his mouth. He was assigned a grave with the wicked, and with the rich in his death, though he had done no violence, nor was any deceit in his mouth. — ISAIAH 53:7,9, C 690 BC

NEW TESTAMENT FULFILLMENT

Then Pilate asked him, "Don't you hear the testimony they are bringing against you?" But Jesus made no reply, not even to a single charge—to the great amazement of the governor.
— MATTHEW 27:13-14, C AD 33

To this you were called, because Christ suffered for you, leaving you an example, that you should follow in his steps. "He committed no sin, and no deceit was found in his mouth." When they hurled their insults at him, he did not retaliate; when he suffered, he made no threats. Instead, he entrusted himself to him who judges justly. He himself bore our sins in his body on the tree, so that we might die to sins and live for righteousness; by his wounds you have been healed. For you were like sheep going astray, but now you have returned to the Shepherd and Overseer of your souls.
— 1 PETER 2:21-25, C AD 66

PIETRO LORENZETTI (1280-1348)

Christ before Pontius Pilate, 1335

Pinacoteca, Vatican Museums, Vatican State. Scala/Art Resource, NY

Christ stands before Pilate with the chief priests looking on. Christ's lips are sealed; he does not utter a word. However, his stance speaks volumes. Staring directly into Pilate's eyes, Christ shows he has no fear of his impending death.

OLD TESTAMENT PROPHECY

Ruthless witnesses come forward; they question me on things I know nothing about. — PSALM 35:11

For wicked and deceitful men have opened their mouths against me; they have spoken against me with lying tongues. With words of hatred they surround me; they attack me without cause. In return for my friendship they accuse me, but I am a man of prayer. — PSALM 109:2-4

NEW TESTAMENT FULFILLMENT

The chief priests and the whole Sanhedrin were looking for false evidence against Jesus so that they could put him to death. But they did not find any, though many false witnesses came forward. — MATTHEW 26:59-60, C AD 33

Many testified falsely against him, but their statements did not agree — MARK 14:56, C AD 33

JAMES JACQUES JOSEPH TISSOT (1836-1902)

'Let Him be Crucified', illustration for 'The Life of Christ', c. 1886-96 (gouache on paperboard)

Brooklyn Museum of Art, New York, USA/Bridgeman Art Library

Christ was innocent; his accusors needed false witnesses to try and make a case, but no case could be made. The Sanhedrin rail at Christ, shaking their fists, pointing their fingers, hurling accusations, but all without merit, without truth.

OLD TESTAMENT PROPHECY

The days are coming," declares the Lord, "when I will raise up to David a righteous Branch, a King who will reign wisely and do what is just and right in the land. In his days, Judah will be saved and Israel will live in safety. This is the name by which he will be called: The Lord Our Righteousness." — JEREMIAH 23:5-6, C 627-585 BC

NEW TESTAMENT FULFILLMENT

Jesus answered, "You would have no power over me if it were not given to you from above." — JOHN 19:11, C AD 33

But the chief priests and the elders persuaded the crowd to ask for Barabbas and to have Jesus executed. "Which of the two do you want me to release to you?" asked the governor. "Barabbas," they answered. "What shall I do then, with Jesus who is called Christ?" Pilate asked. They all answered, Crucify him!" "Why? What crime has he committed?" asked Pilate. But they shouted all the louder, "Crucify him!" When Pilate saw that he was getting nowhere, but that instead an uproar was starting, he took water and washed his hands in front of the crowd. "I am innocent of this man's blood," he said. "It is your responsibility!" — MATTHEW 27:20-24. C AD 33

JACOPO TINTORETTO (1518-1594)

Christ before Pilate, 1566-1567

Scuola Grande di S. Rocco, Venice, Italy. Scala/Art Resource, NY

"While Pilate was sitting on the judge's seat, his wife sent him this message: 'Don't have anything to do with that innocent man, for I have suffered a great deal today in a dream because of him.' " (Matthew 27:19) Tintoretto depicts Christ standing before Pilate. Not wanting to be blamed for Christ's death, Pilate literally washes his hands of Christ's innocent blood. Note the washbasin and water pitcher as seen in Van Eyck's *Annunciation*. Tintoretto has obscured this setting with dark shadows, anticipating the gloom of the sinister events to come. Christ is set apart from the overcast environment as he is bathed in a beam of light, a ray of hope.

OLD TESTAMENT PROPHECY

I offered my back to those who beat me, my cheeks to those who pulled out my beard; I did not hide my face from mocking and spitting. — ISAIAH 50:6, C 690 BC

NEW TESTAMENT FULFILLMENT

Then he released Barabbas to them. But he had Jesus flogged, and handed him over to be crucified. Then the governor's soldiers took Jesus into the Praetorium and gathered the whole company of soldiers around him. They stripped him and put a scarlet robe on him, and then twisted together a crown of thorns and set it on his head. They put a staff in his right hand and knelt in front of him and mocked him. "Hail, King of the Jews!" they said. They spit on him, and took the staff and struck him on the head again and again. — MATTHEW 27:26-30 , C AD 33

JAIME HUGUET (1414-C.1492)

The Flagellation of Christ. 1455-60
Antependium painted for the cathedral of Barcelona.
Oil on polar wood. 102 x 210 cm.

Louvre, Paris, France. Scala/Art Resource, NY

Pilate looks on as Christ is tied to a column, beaten. Pilate's wife stands next to him urging him to have nothing to do with this innocent man. One angel wipes blood from Christ's face as two others catch his blood in golden chalices, symbolizing the precious blood of Christ shed for many, for the forgiveness of sins.

103

OLD TESTAMENT PROPHECY

The days are coming," declares the Lord, "when I will raise up to David a righteous branch, a King who will reign wisely and do what is just and right in the land."

— JEREMIAH 23:5, C 627-585 BC

NEW TESTAMENT FULFILLMENT

Pilate then went back inside the palace, summoned Jesus and asked him, "Are you the king of the Jews?" "Is that your own idea," Jesus asked, "or did others talk to you about me?" "Am I a Jew?" Pilate replied. "It was your people and your chief priests who handed you over to me. What is it you have done?" Jesus said, "My kingdom is not of this world. If it were, my servants would fight to prevent my arrest by the Jews. But now my kingdom is from another place." "You are a king, then!" said Pilate. Jesus answered, "You are right in saying I am a king. In fact, for this reason I was born, and for this I came into the world, to testify to the truth. Everyone on the side of truth listens to me."

— JOHN 18:33-37, C AD 33

ANTONIO CISERI (1821-1891)

Ecco Homo

Palazzo Pitti, Florence, Italy. Scala/Art Resource/NY

Again we see Christ and Pilate together. Pilate points to Christ, shouting "Ecco Homo!"— Behold the man! The woman to the right of Pilate is his wife, who warned against this display.

OLD TESTAMENT PROPHECY

You know how I am scorned, disgraced and shamed; all my enemies are before you. — PSALM 69:19

I am an object of scorn to my accusers; when they see me, they shake their heads. — PSALM 109:25

NEW TESTAMENT FULFILLMENT

They stripped him and put a scarlet robe on him. — MATTHEW 27:28 , C AD 33

And those who were passing by were hurling abuse at him, wagging their heads. . . — MATTHEW 27:39, C AD 33

EL GRECO (DOMENICO THEOTOCOPULI) (1541-1614)
Despoiling of Christ, 1583-1584

Alte Pinakothek, Munich, Germany, Scala/Art Resource, NY

El Greco has captured the moment that Christ, surrounded by a mocking crowd, is draped with a robe of red—traditionally the color of royalty. At Christ's feet we see a laborer drilling holes into the timbers of the cross. To the left Mary looks away in sorrow. Christ seems unfazed by the commotion around him, as he looks up to the heavens foreseeing his ascension.

OLD TESTAMENT PROPHECY

All who see me mock me; they hurl insults, shaking their heads. — PSALM 22:7-8

NEW TESTAMENT FULFILLMENT

They spit on him, and took the staff and struck him on the head again and again. After they mocked him, they took off the robe and put his own clothes on him. Then they led him away to crucify him. — MATTHEW 27:30-31, C AD 33

FRA ANGELICO (GUIDO DI PIETRO) (1387-1455)

The Mocking of Christ, 1440-1441

Museo di San Marco, Florence, Italy. Scala/Art Resource, NY

Fra Angelico appears ahead of his time with this seemingly contemporary depiction of the mockery of Christ. Surrealistically, a head floats to the left of Christ, spitting in his face, while to the right we see a pair of hands, which are both slapping Christ and mocking his actions. An anguished Mother Mary and a Dominican scholar sit at Christ's feet.

The halo above Christ's head resembles the Banner of Resurrection. Although Christ is blindfolded, we still see his eyes. Equally, it is expected that he can "see us." The unsuccessful blindfold and the Banner of Resurrection both foreshadow Christ's destiny.

THE MUTILATION CAUSED BY THE VIOLENCE OF THE SOLDIERS

OLD TESTAMENT PROPHECY

Just as there were many who were appalled at him—his appearance was so disfigured beyond that of any man, and his form marred beyond human likeness. — ISAIAH 52:14, C 740-680 BC

The sovereign Lord has opened my ears, and I have not been rebellious; I have not drawn back. I offered my back to those who beat me, my cheeks to those who pulled out my beard; I did not hide my face from mocking and spitting. — ISAIAH 50:5-6, C 740-680 BC

NEW TESTAMENT FULFILLMENT

Then they spit in his face and struck him with their fists. Others slapped him and said, "Prophesy to us, Christ. Who hit you?" — MATTHEW 26:67-68, C AD 33

Then some began to spit at him; they blindfolded him, struck him with their fists, and said, "Prophesy!" And the guards took him and beat him. — MARK 14:65, C AD 33

Jesus knew what would happen to him, but he submitted to God's will anyway so that our sins could be forgiven.

MATHIAS GRUENEWALD (1455-1528)

Detail of Entombment (Christ upper torso), predella panel from the Isenheim altarpiece, 1515

Musee Unterlinden, Colmar, France. Giraudon/Art Resource, NY

Gruenewald truly envisioned the brutal beatings that Christ withstood. Through wounds too numerous to count, the artist has presented only a glimpse of the pain Christ endured.

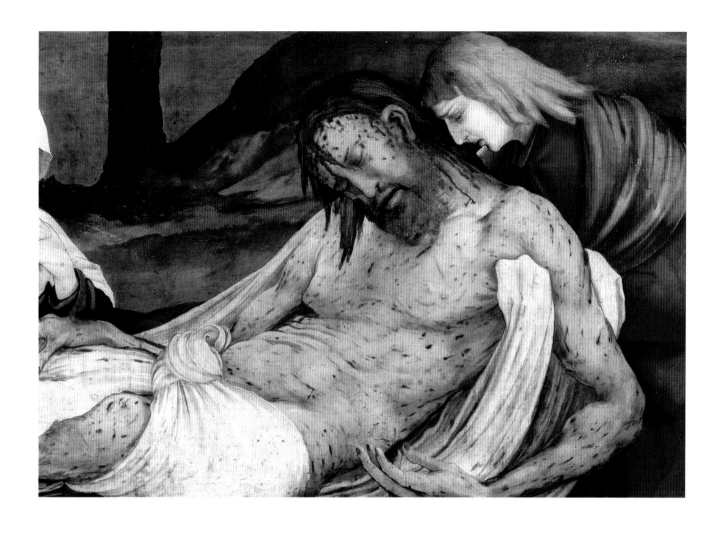

O L D   T E S T A M E N T   P R O P H E C Y

T hose who hate me without reason outnumber the hairs of my head; many are my enemies without cause, those who seek to destroy me. — PSALM 69:4

N E W   T E S T A M E N T   F U L F I L L M E N T

B ut this is to fulfill what is written in their Law: "They hated me without reason." — JOHN 15:25, C AD 33

Then Pilate announced to the chief priests and the crowd, "I find no basis for a charge against this man." — LUKE 23:4, C AD 33

Jesus knew every prophecy had to be fulfilled, and he knew the pain and torment that would befall him.

S I M O N E   M A R T I N I   (1 2 8 4 - 1 3 4 4)

The Road to Calvary, 1340-1344

Louvre, Paris, France. Scala/Art Resource, NY

Simone Martini takes us down the road from the temple. As Christ walks to Calvary, he is surrounded by people punching, pulling on him, and yelling at him. Repulsive persecutors have encircled him. The two small children in the lower right corner are not old enough to understand uninhibited abhorrence, yet look at the disparagement on their faces. It is obvious they have learned this loathing from the fury and hatred around them. They hate Jesus without cause.

113

49

CHRIST IS WEAK FROM FASTING

OLD TESTAMENT PROPHECY

My knees give way from fasting; my body is thin and gaunt." — PSALM 109:24

NEW TESTAMENT FULFILLMENT

At the Last Supper, Christ stated to his apostles:

. . . I tell you, I will not drink of this fruit of the vine from now on until that day when I drink it anew with you in my Father's kingdom." — MATTHEW 26:29, C AD 33

Christ ate nothing after this Passover meal. Later he was interrogated, beaten and whipped throughout the night. He became too weak to carry the cross.

As they led him away, they seized Simon from Cyrene, who was on his way in from the country, and put the cross on him and made him carry it behind Jesus. — LUKE 23:26, C AD 33

RAPHAEL (RAFFAELLO SANZIO OF URBINO) (1483-1520)

Christ Falls on the Way to Calvary, 1517

Prado, Madrid, Spain/Bridgeman Art Library

Christ has suffered intense pain and is very weak at this point. However, Raphael has painted Christ with utmost dignity and pride. Seemingly unworried about his own pain or even his impending death, he turns back to give a reassuring look to his grieving mother.

50

CHRIST IS THE SACRIFICIAL LAMB OF GOD

OLD TESTAMENT PROPHECY

Then Moses summoned all the elders of Israel and said to them, "Go at once and select the animals for your family and slaughter the Passover lamb." — EXODUS 12:21, C 1450 BC

He was oppressed and afflicted, yet he did not open his mouth; he was led like a lamb to the slaughter, and as a sheep before her shearers is silent, so he did not open his mouth. — ISAIAH 53:7, C 690 BC

NEW TESTAMENT FULFILLMENT

The next day John saw Jesus coming toward him and said, "Look, the Lamb of God, who takes away the sin of the world!" — JOHN 1:29, C AD 26

Jewish law said the sin offering had to be a male perfect in every way without a single bone broken. Jesus was this perfect sacrifice.

JAN VAN EYCK (C. 1390-1441)

Adoration of the Mystic Lamb, detail from the Ghent altarpiece, 1432

Cathedral St. Bavo, Ghent, Belgium. Scala/Art Resource, NY

The Lamb has long been an icon for Christ and the sacrifice. The Van Eycks' representation stands alone on the sacrificial altar. Blood from a wound in his chest pours into a golden chalice, signifying the blood of Christ as the Eucharistic wine. On either side of the altar angels hold symbols of Christ's crucifixion, his cross and the column to which he was bound when beaten. In front of the altar is the baptismal fountain of life, which is cleansing the sins of the world. The scene is bathed in a radiant light emanating from the dove of the Holy Spirit.

51

THE CRUCIFIXION

The way in which Christ would die was foretold in the scriptures more than seven hundred years before it took place. His hands and feet would be pierced as he was nailed to a cross. It is interesting to note the Jewish method of capital punishment was by stoning.

OLD TESTAMENT PROPHECIES

But he was pierced for our transgressions, he was crushed for our iniquities; the punishment that brought us peace was upon him, and by his wounds we are healed. — ISAIAH 53:5 , C 690 BC

Dogs have surrounded me; a band of evil men has encircled me, they have pierced my hands and my feet. — PSALM 22:16

NEW TESTAMENT FULFILLMENT

Finally Pilate handed him over to them to be crucified. So the soldiers took charge of Jesus. Carrying his own cross, he went out to the place of the skull (which in Aramaic is called Golgotha). Here they crucified him, and with him two others—one on each side and Jesus in the middle.
— JOHN 19:16-18, C AD 33

ANDREA MANTEGNA (1431-1506)

Calvary. Central panel of predella from the San Zeno altarpiece, 1457-1459

Louvre, Paris, France/Erich Lessing/Art Resource, NY

Note the bloodstained skull at the base of Christ's cross. This skull represents Adam. Christ's blood drips upon it, symbolizing forgiveness of original sin. The penitent thief on Christ's right turns toward him in sunlight; he is coming to the light of Christ. The people below him include the grieving Mary and John. In the background the rich countryside abounds with greenery. To Christ's left is the unrepentant thief. He is turned away from Christ and almost disappears into the shadows, showing that his destiny is darkness. The evil ones below the thief are the soldiers responsible for Christ's death. The land behind is barren and desolate.

INRI

OLD TESTAMENT PROPHECY

They divide my garments among them and cast lots for my clothing. — PSALM 22:18

NEW TESTAMENT FULFILLMENT

When they had crucified him, they divided up his clothes by casting lots. — MATTHEW 27:35

ANDREA MANTEGNA (1431-1506)

Detail of Calvary. Central panel of predella from the San Zeno altarpiece, 1457-1459

Louvre, Paris, France, Erich Lessing/Art Resource, NY

In this detail of Mantegna's Crucifixion, the soldiers are casting lots (throwing dice) for Christ's clothing. Here we can see firsthand the strict attention to detail paid by Mantegna. The crisp modeling of the soldiers' bodies is almost sculptural. In fact he follows an obsession with the human body much like that of Michelangelo.

OLD TESTAMENT PROPHECY

Therefore I will give him a portion among the great, and he will divide the spoils with the strong, because he poured out his life unto death, and was numbered with the transgressors. For he bore the sin of many, and made intercession for the transgressors. — ISAIAH 53:12, C 690 BC

NEW TESTAMENT FULFILLMENT

It is written: "And he was numbered with the transgressors"; and I tell you that this must be fulfilled in me. Yes, what is written about me is reaching its fulfillment. — LUKE 22:37, C AD 33

When they came to the place called the Skull, there they crucified him, along with the criminals—one on his right, the other on his left. — LUKE 23:33, C AD 33

One of the criminals believed in God the Son.

One of the criminals who hung there hurled insults at him: "Aren't you the Christ? Save yourself and us!" But the other criminal rebuked him. "Don't you fear God," he said, "since you are under the same sentence?" We are punished justly, for we are getting what our deeds deserve. But this man has done nothing wrong." Then he said, "Jesus, remember me when you come into your kingdom." Jesus answered him, "I tell you the truth, today you will be with me in paradise." — LUKE 23:39-43, C AD 33

FRA ANGELICO (GUIDO DI PIETRO) (1387-1455)

Crucifixion, 1441-1442

Museo di San Marco, Florence, Italy. Scala/Art Resource, NY

The moment of darkness has just arrived and Fra Angelico places us directly in front of Christ and the thieves. To Christ's right is the penitent thief, turning to Christ in adoration, while under him is the devastated Mary supported by the other Marys and John the Baptist, present here though already killed. To Christ's left hangs the unrepentant thief, staring off in the distance without emotion. This placement of the thieves is a common occurrence. Quite often artists portray all that is good on Christ's right and all that is evil on his left.

OLD TESTAMENT PROPHECY

My friends and companions avoid me because of my wounds; my neighbors stay far away. — PSALMS 38:11

NEW TESTAMENT FULFILLMENT

And all his acquaintances, and the women that followed him from Galilee, stood afar off, beholding these things. — LUKE 23:49, C AD 33

HUBERT VAN EYCK (1366-1426)

The Crucifixion (oil on panel), detail

Ca'd'Oro, Venice, Italy/Bridgeman Art Library

Again we see the skull at the bottom of the cross. As Mary laments her dead son, St. John comforts her. However, they are all who remain at this scene. Just as described in the New Testament, all of Christ's acquaintances stand far off. Behind Mary, Mary Magdelene cloaks her head in grief. All of the other spectators are departing. Only Mary and John maintain their positions. Even Mary Magdalene begins to take her leave. Blood from Christ's pierced side drips down the cross toward the skull, pointing again to redemption from sin.

OLD TESTAMENT PROPHECY

After the suffering of his soul, he will see the light of life and be satisfied; by his knowledge my righteous servant will justify many, and he will bear their iniquities. Therefore I will give him a portion among the great, and he will divide the spoils with the strong, because he poured out his life unto death, and was numbered with the transgressors. For he bore the sin of many, and made intercession for the transgressors. — ISAIAH 53:11-12, C 690 BC

NEW TESTAMENT FULFILLMENT

Jesus said, "Father, forgive them, for they do not know what they are doing." — LUKE 23:34, C AD 33

But because Jesus lives forever, he has a permanent priesthood. Therefore he is able to save completely those who come to God through him, because he always lives to intercede for them. — HEBREWS 7:24-25, C AD 64-68

EL GRECO (DOMENICO THEOTOCOPULI) (1541-1614)

Crucifixion (oil on canvas)

Casa y Museo del Greco, Toledo, Spain/Bridgeman Art Library

Even during his moments of greatest pain, Christ looks up to the heavens in prayer. In spite of all that the torturers have done to him, Christ still forgives them and prays for them thus paving the path for forgiveness and redemption not only of the original sin, but for all of our sins.

127

OLD TESTAMENT PROPHECY

My strength is dried up like a potsherd, and my tongue sticks to the roof of my mouth; you lay me in the dust of death." — PSALMS 22:15

NEW TESTAMENT FULFILLMENT

Later, knowing that all was now completed, and so that the Scripture would be fulfilled, Jesus said, "I am thirsty." — JOHN 19:28, C AD 33

GRAHAM SUTHERLAND (1903-1980)

The Crucifixion, 1946 (oil on hardboard)

Saint Matthew's Church, Northampton, Northamptonshire, UK/Bridgeman Art Library

Sutherland's influence for this work came from photographs showing the suffering of prisoners in Nazi concentration camps, including Auschwitz. This frail image of Christ explicitly defines his lack of nourishment. His stomach appears so gaunt he seems incapable of eating. However, something to drink is not out of the question. His listless body hangs as he attempts to lift his head for any refreshment. Of this work, Sutherland said, "The Crucifixion idea interested me because it has a duality which has always fascinated me. It is the most tragic of all themes yet inherent in it is the promise of salvation. It is a symbol of the precarious balanced moment, the hair's breadth between black and white." (*Graham Sutherland* by Ronald Alley, The Tate Gallery, 1982)

57

CHRIST IS GIVEN VINEGAR TO DRINK; HIS THIRST IS QUENCHED WITH BITTERNESS

OLD TESTAMENT PROPHECY

They put gall in my food and gave me vinegar for my thirst." — PSALMS 69:21

NEW TESTAMENT FULFILLMENT

A jar of wine vinegar was there, so they soaked a sponge in it, put the sponge on a stalk of the hyssop plant, and lifted it to Jesus' lips. — JOHN 19:29, C AD 33

FRA ANGELICO (GUIDO DI PIETRO) (C. 1387-1455)

The Crucifixion with the Sponge-Bearer, 1442 (fresco)

Museo di San Marco dell'Angelico, Florence, Italy/Bridgeman Art Library

To the right of Christ a centurion lifts a stick up to him. Attached to the end of that stick is a sponge which has been soaked in vinegar. Below Christ, his mother and Mary Magdalene kneel in pity.

58

CHRIST'S INTENSE, LONELY CRY
IN THE HOUR OF HIS SUFFERING

*Of everything Christ had to endure, this brief separation from God the Father was perhaps the hardest.
To complete the sacrifice, Jesus had to die. He also had to experience the severing of his spiritual connection to
God the Father.*

"And being in anguish, he prayed more earnestly and his sweat was like drops of blood falling to
the ground."— LUKE 22:44, C AD 33

He feared the pain and torture and crucifixion, but much more the separation from God the Father.

OLD TESTAMENT PROPHECY

My God, my God, why have you forsaken me? Why are you so far from saving me, so far from
the words of my groaning? — PSALM 22:1

NEW TESTAMENT FULFILLMENT

About the ninth hour Jesus cried out in a loud voice, "Eloi, Eloi, lama sabachthani?"—which
means, "My God, my God, why have you forsaken me?"— MATTHEW 27:46 , C AD 33

FOLLOWER OF PETER PAUL RUBENS (1577-1640)

The Crucifixion

Wallace Collection, London, UK/Bridgeman Art Library

The tortured Jesus looks up to God to ask why he has been forsaken. Jesus knew this separation
would be the most painful part of his tribulation. Darkness has fallen over the land. Clearly this must be
the sixth hour. Rubens employs this dark backdrop as a powerful contrast to Christ's radiating body.
This chiaroscuro technique provides a tension as intense as Christ's cry must have been. Fixed to the
cross over Christ's head is the notice Pilate inscribed with the words "Jesus of Nazareth, King of the
Jews" written in Hebrew, Greek, and Latin.

OLD TESTAMENT PROPHECIES

I am poured out like water, and all my bones are out of joint. My heart has turned to wax; it has melted away within me." — PSALM 22:14

Scorn has broken my heart and has left me helpless; I looked for sympathy, but there was none, for comforters, but I found none. — PSALM 69:20

NEW TESTAMENT FULFILLMENT

Instead, one of the soldiers pierced Jesus' side with a spear, bringing a sudden flow of blood and water. — JOHN 19:34 , C AD 33

MATHIAS GRUENEWALD (1455-1528)

Crucifixion, with side panels of Saints Sebastian and Anthony, Isenheim Altarpiece, closed, 1515

Musee Unterlinden, Colmar, France. Giraudon/Art Resource, NY

Gruenewald was commissioned to execute this altarpiece for the Monastic Hospital of St. Anthony of Isenheim. It became a gruesome reminder to the patient that another had suffered more than they. The hospital became a haven for those afflicted with ergotism or "St. Anthony's Fire". Many times the only way to save a patient from this disease was to amputate the affected arm or leg. Christ is placed off center in the piece, such that when the altarpiece is opened, Christ's arm is "severed."

The outer right section of the painting houses St. Anthony, the patron saint of the hospital. St. Anthony is credited with curing disease and warding off evil spirits. On the outer left section is St. Sebastian, who was called to bring about miraculous cures of the plague.

In the center section, John the Evangelist is shown on the left side of the cross supporting Mary while Mary Magdalene laments. On the right side of the cross is John the Baptist pointing to Christ. By inserting the already martyred John the Baptist, the artist has made use of a powerful illusion. With the sacrificial lamb at his feet, blood dripping into the golden chalice, it is as though John eternally points to Christ as he did by the Jordan River, "Behold the lamb of God who takes away the sins of the world." (John 1:29) The Latin inscription flowing from John's mouth is translated as, "It is fitting that he increase and I diminish." The swiftly flowing River Jordan signifies the healing of the soul. In addition, Gruenewald interprets the river for its power in healing the body, reflecting the growing interest in hydrotherapy in the Middle Ages.

JESUS COMMITS HIMSELF TO GOD
WITH A CRY OF TRIUMPH AND VICTORY

OLD TESTAMENT PROPHECY

Into your hands I commit my spirit; redeem me, O Lord, the God of truth. — PSALMS 31:5

NEW TESTAMENT FULFILLMENT

Jesus called out with a loud voice, "Father, into your hands I commit my spirit." When he had said this, he breathed his last. — LUKE 23:46, C AD 33

The death of Christ from a medical perspective is analyzed in an excerpt from "The Crucifixation of Jesus: The Passion of Christ from a Medical Point of View" by C. Truman Davis, M.D., M.S. The title contains a contraction of the two words crucifixion and asphyxiation. Davis writes, "Hours of this limitless pain, cycles of twisting, joint-rending cramps, intermittent partial asphyxiation, searing pain as tissue is torn from His lacerated back as he moves up and down against the rough timber; then another agony begins. A deep crushing pain deep in the chest as the pericardium slowly fills with serum and begins to compress the heart. . . . It is now almost over–the loss of tissue fluids has reached a critical level – the compressed heart is struggling to pump heavy, thick, sluggish blood into the tissues–the tortured lungs are making dehydrated tissues send their flood of stimuli to the brain. . . .His mission of atonement has been completed. Finally he can allow His body to die. . . . With one last surge of strength, he once again presses His torn feet against the nail, straightens His legs, takes a deeper breath, and utters His seventh and last cry, 'Father, into Thy hands I commit my spirit.' "

Christ knew every detail of his death before it happened.

LUCAS CRANACH THE ELDER (1472-1553)

Crucifixion, 1503

Alte Pinakothek, Munich, Germany. Scala/Art Resource, NY

Hanging over Christ is a representation of the same sign ordered by Pilate. However, frequently in Renaissance art only the Latin is inscribed: Iesus Nazarenus Rex Iudaeorum, abbreviated as INRI. We see many symbols we have seen in similar works—the skull, the descending darkness. Mary falls into the arms of St. John. The repentant thief turns toward Christ, the unrepentant turns away. Look closely at the bruising on the shins of the unrepentant thief. Cranach has depicted him as the only one of the three whose legs have been broken.

DARKNESS COMES OVER THE LAND

God the Father made it clear this was God the Son by fulfilling the prophecy of the sun going down at noon. The sixth hour mentioned in Mark and Luke is noon. The hours start at daylight.

OLD TESTAMENT PROPHECY

In that day," declares the Sovereign Lord, "I will make the sun go down at noon and darken the earth in broad daylight." — AMOS 8:9, C 760 BC

NEW TESTAMENT FULFILLMENT

At the sixth hour darkness came over the whole land until the ninth hour. — MARK 15:33, C AD 33

It was now about the sixth hour, and darkness came over the whole land until the ninth hour, for the sun stopped shining. — LUKE 23:44, C AD 33

LIMBOURG BROTHERS (15TH CENTURY)

Darkness at Christ's Death

Musee Conde, Chantilly, France/Giraudon/Art Resource, NY

This indeed is the moment of darkness. As Christ is breathing his last breath, the Lord is blessing him from heaven. In the upper corners of this work, the sun and moon compete for their places in the sky. At the base of the cross, the converted centurion beats his heart as he exclaims, "Surely he was the son of God." (Matthew 27:54) The Virgin Mary collapses into the arms of John.

We see three roundels outside of the main picture frame. The upper right sphere contains an astronomer scanning the sky for an explanation of the sudden eclipse. Below him we see the veil of the temple ripping in two. The roundel on the bottom of this illuminated manuscript portrays the bodies of the saints who had "fallen asleep" being resurrected.

Old Testament Prophecy

On this mountain he will destroy the shroud that enfolds all peoples, the sheet that covers all nations; he will swallow up death forever. The Sovereign Lord will wipe away the tears from all faces; he will remove the disgrace of his people from all the earth. The Lord has spoken.
—— ISAIAH 25:7-8, BETWEEN 734 AND 730 BC

Make a curtain of blue, purple and scarlet yarn and finely twisted linen, with cherubim worked into it by a skilled craftsman. Hang it with gold hooks on four posts of acacia wood overlaid with gold and standing on four silver bases. Hang the curtain from the clasps and place the ark of the Testimony behind the curtain. The curtain will separate the Holy Place from the Most Holy Place.
—— EXODUS 26:31-33

New Testament Fulfillment

And when Jesus had cried out again in a loud voice, he gave up his spirit. At that moment the curtain of the temple was torn in two from top to bottom. The earth shook and the rocks split.
—— MATTHEW 27:51-50, C AD 33

Therefore, brothers, since we have confidence to enter the Most Holy Place by the blood of Jesus, by a new and living way opened for us through the curtain, that is, his body, and since we have a great priest over the house of God, let us draw near to God with a sincere heart in full assurance of faith, having our hearts sprinkled to cleanse us from a guilty conscience and having our bodies washed with pure water. —— HEBREW 10:19-23, C AD 64

Limbourg Brothers (15th century)

Darkness at Christ's Death, Detail

Musee Conde, Chantilly, France, Giraudon/Art Resource, NY

This detail from a painting by the Limbourg brothers shows the curtain of the temple torn. The veil of the temple was erected in order to divide the Holy Place from the Most Holy Place. Specific requirements were established in Exodus as to how this holy veil must be made and suspended. The Most Holy Place, where the Ark of the Covenant was housed, was considered to be a room emanating with the direct presence of God. Only the highest of priests were allowed to enter. At the moment of Jesus' death, the veil tears, therefore giving access to the Most Holy, God, to all people through Jesus Christ.

EVEN THE ROMAN GUARDS BELIEVE THAT JESUS IS THE SON OF GOD

OLD TESTAMENT PROPHECY

I, the Lord, have called you in righteousness; I will take hold of your hand. I will keep you and will make you be a covenant for the people and a light to the Gentiles, to open eyes that are blind, to free captives from prison and to release from the dungeon those who sit in darkness. — ISAIAH 42:6-7

NEW TESTAMENT FULFILLMENT

When the centurion and those with him who were guarding Jesus saw the earthquake and all that had happened, they were terrified, and exclaimed, "Surely he was the Son of God!"
— MATTHEW 27:54, CA AD 33

The same guards who beat Christ and mocked him, after seeing all of the things that happened while he was on the cross, knew he truly was the Son of God. This is symbolic of his universal acceptance by the Gentiles.

CARLO CRIVELLI (C. 1430/35-1495)

The Crucifixion, central left hand predella panel from the San Silvestro polyptych, 1468, tempera on panel

San Lorenzo y San Silvestro, Massa Fermana/Bridgeman Art Library

145

65

CHRIST, LIKE THE PASSOVER LAMB, WILL HAVE NOT A BONE BROKEN

OLD TESTAMENT PROPHECIES

It must be eaten inside one house; take none of the meat outside the house. Do not break any of the bones. — EXODUS 12:46, C 1450 BC

A righteous man may have many troubles, but the Lord delivers him from them all; he protects all his bones, not one of them will be broken. — PSALM 34:19-20

NEW TESTAMENT FULFILLMENT

But when they came to Jesus and found that he was already dead, they did not break his legs. Instead, one of the soldiers pierced Jesus' side with a spear, bringing a sudden flow of blood and water. The man who saw it has given testimony, and his testimony is true. He knows that he tells the truth, and he testifies so that you also may believe. These things happened so that the scripture would be fulfilled: "Not one of his bones will be broken." — JOHN 19:33-36, C AD 33

Under Jewish law, the sacrificial Passover lamb must be flawless, with no bones broken. To be a perfect sacrifice, Jesus had to be whole in every way; with all bones fully intact. A crucified person was not allowed to be left hanging on the Sabbath. The soldiers would inspect the criminals the day before. If the criminals were still alive, their legs were broken. This forced all the weight of their bodies onto their arms, compressing their lungs and causing suffocation, thus hastening death. When the soldiers reached Jesus, they pierced his side. Seeing the water and blood, they knew he was already dead. They did not break his legs. He remained the perfect sacrifice.

GIOVANNI BATTISTA ROSSO FIORENTINO (1494-1540)

The Descent From the Cross, 1521, panel

Pinacoteca, Volterra, Italy/Bridgeman Art Library

The nails that pierced Christ's body have been removed. Joseph of Arimathea, perched on top of the cross, supervises the descent. Christ's limp body is shown collapsing into the arms of Nicodemus. His legs do not show the bruising often seen on the broken legs of the unrepentant thief. At the base of the cross Mary Magdalene kneels over to comfort the Virgin while John the Evangelist turns away from the wretched scene in misery.

147

OLD TESTAMENT PROPHECY

He was assigned a grave with the wicked, and with the rich in his death, though he had done no violence, nor was any deceit in his mouth. — ISAIAH 53:9, C 690 BC

NEW TESTAMENT FULFILLMENT

As evening approached, there came a rich man from Arimathea, named Joseph, who had himself become a disciple of Jesus. Going to Pilate, he asked for Jesus' body, and Pilate ordered that it be given to him. Joseph took the body, wrapped it in a clean linen cloth, and placed it in his own new tomb that he had cut out of the rock. He rolled a big stone in front of the entrance to the tomb and went away. — MATTHEW 27:57-60, C AD 33

PETER PAUL RUBENS (1577-1640)

The Entombment, c. 1615-16 (panel)

Courtauld Gallery, London, UK/Bridgeman Art Library

Joseph of Arimathea was a very wealthy man, a very prominent figure in the community. He had previously had his own sepulcher carved in a nearby cave. Here, the mourners have entered the cave. Joseph and Nicodemus carefully lower Christ's body into the tomb. Mary Magdalene washes Christ's feet.

The Messiah will die not for himself

Old Testament Prophecies

After the sixty-two "sevens," the Anointed One will be cut off and will have nothing.
— DANIEL 9:26, C 538 BC

But he was pierced for our transgressions, he was crushed for our iniquities; the punishment that brought us peace was upon him, and by his wounds we are healed. We all, like sheep, have gone astray, each of us has turned to his own way; and the Lord has laid on him the iniquity of us all.
— ISAIAH 53:5-6, C 690 BC

New Testament Fulfillment

Then one of them, named Caiaphas, who was high priest that year, spoke up, "You know nothing at all! You do not realize that it is better for you that one man die for the people than that the whole nation perish." He did not say this on his own, but as high priest that year he prophesied that Jesus would die for the Jewish nation, and not only for that nation but also for the scattered children of God, to bring them together and make them one. — JOHN 11:49-52, C AD 33

It is interesting that the high priest Caiaphas said just what was true. Jesus would die for the Jewish nation and for all who believed.

Michelangelo Buonarroti (1475-1564)

Pieta, 1499

St. Peter's Basilica, Vatican State. Scala/Art Resource, NY

Michelangelo was ridiculed over this glorious work. First, he completed *Pieta* when he was only twenty-four. No one could believe that such a young man could produce such a graceful masterpiece. Reinforcement from Michelangelo's adversaries came from the fact that he never signed his work. Over time he tired of the constant battle to claim his work; he eventually signed his name in the ribbon of Mary's robe. This is the only piece ever signed by the artist.

The next discrepancy Michelangelo faced with *Pieta* was Mary's age. At the time Christ died, Mary would have been approximately fifty years old. Yet, in the sculpture she appears much younger. When ridiculed for not portraying Mary's actual age, Michelangelo explained that a pure virgin will maintain her appearance of youth much longer than any other woman. Michelangelo portrays Jesus' dead body in the lap of the woman who gave him birth.

As prophesied in the Old Testament and by Jesus several times before his death, he would be raised up in three days.

OLD TESTAMENT PROPHECY

Because you will not abandon me to the grave, nor will you let your Holy One see decay. — PSALM 16:10

NEW TESTAMENT FULFILLMENT

Brothers, I can tell you confidently that the patriarch David died and was buried, and his tomb is here to this day. But he was a prophet and knew that God had promised him on oath that he would place one of his descendants on his throne. Seeing what was ahead, he spoke of the resurrection of the Christ, that he was not abandoned to the grave, nor did his body see decay.

— ACTS 2:29-31, C AD 33

"Don't be alarmed," he said. "You are looking for Jesus the Nazarene, who was crucified. He has risen! He is not here. See the place where they laid him." — MARK 16:6, C AD 33

ANDREA MANTEGNA (1431-1506)

Resurrection of Christ

Musee des Beaux-Arts, Tours, France. Musee Municipal, Tours, France. Scala/Art Resource, NY

Christ carries the Banner of Resurrection. The flag with the red cross is symbolic of victory over death. The guarding soldiers have fallen back in awe and fear of the intense light beaming from Christ. Present on this dessicated cave are new trees which have sprung to life in accompaniment of Christ's everlasting life.

Before his death Christ told his disciples:

"But after I have risen, I will go ahead of you into Galilee". — MATTHEW 26:32, C AD 33

Then after his death:

The angel said to the women, "Do not be afraid, for I know that you are looking for Jesus, who was crucified. He is not here; he has risen, just as he said. Come and see the place where he lay. Then go quickly and tell his disciples: 'He has risen from the dead and is going ahead of you into Galilee. There you will see him.' Now I have told you." — MATTHEW 28:5-7, C AD 33

Doubting Thomas

After Peter and John had seen Jesus, they told Thomas:

"We have seen the Lord!" But he said to them, "Unless I see the nail marks in his hands and put my finger where the nails were, and put my hand into his side, I will not believe it." A week later his disciples were in the house again, and Thomas was with them. Though the doors were locked, Jesus came and stood among them and said, "Peace be with you!" Then he said to Thomas, "Put your finger here; see my hands. Reach out your hand and put it into my side. Stop doubting and believe." Thomas said to him, "My Lord and my God!" — JOHN 20:25-28, C AD 33

Jesus' resurrection was seen by many people

Paul stated in I Corinthians that:

"Christ died for our sins according to the Scriptures, that he was buried, that he was raised on the third day according to the Scriptures, and that he appeared to Peter, and then to the Twelve. After that, he appeared to more than five hundred of the brothers at the same time, most of whom are still living . . ." — I CORINTHIANS 15:3-6

F O L L O W E R   O F   C A R A V A G G I O   (1 5 7 3 - 1 6 1 0)

Detail of Doubting of St. Thomas, 1601-1602

Vecchia Posta, Florence, Italy/Alinari Art Resource, NY

Caravaggio reveals the moment between Thomas' doubt and his revelation. He leans over to touch Christ, not believing the truth of his resurrection. He actually sticks his finger into the hole of Christ's pierced side. Caravaggio's play of light depicts the entire scene as bathed in shadows, except for Christ. The bright light reflected from his body and soul correspond to the instant of enlightenment for Thomas.

THE ASCENSION

OLD TESTAMENT PROPHECY

In my vision at night I looked, and there before me was one like a son of man, coming with the clouds of heaven. He approached the Ancient of Days and was led into his presence.
— DANIEL 7:13, C 545 BC

NEW TESTAMENT FULFILLMENT

He said to them: "It is not for you to know the times or dates the Father has set by his own authority. But you will receive power when the Holy Spirit comes on you; and you will be my witnesses in Jerusalem, and in all Judea and Samaria, and to the ends of the earth." After he said this, he was taken up before their very eyes, and a cloud hid him from their sight. — ACTS 1:7-9, C AD 33

REMBRANDT VAN RIJN (1606-1669)

The Ascension of Christ, 1636

Alte Pinakothek, Munich, Germany. Scala/Art Resource, NY

This ethereal painting by Rembrandt shows the amazing moment of Christ ascending into heaven. The eleven apostles fall back in astonishment as the angels guide Christ to the Lord. There is a distinct division in the picture field between heaven and Earth which exemplifies Christ's leaving the darkness of this world and entering the light of the heavenly realm as he ascends.

OLD TESTAMENT PROPHECY

Nations will come to your light, and kings to the brightness of your dawn. — ISAIAH 60:3, C 690 BC

It is too small a thing for you to be my servant to restore the tribes of Jacob and bring back those from Israel I have kept. I will also make you a light for the Gentiles, that you may bring my salvation to the ends of the earth. — ISAIAH 49:6, C 690 BC

The Lord is God and has made his Light to shine on us. — PSALM 118:27

NEW TESTAMENT FULFILLMENT

When Jesus spoke again to the people, he said, "I am the light of the world. Whoever follows me will never walk in darkness, but will have the light of life." — JOHN 8:12, C AD 32

The true light that gives light to every man was coming into the world. He was in the world, and though the world was made through him, the world did not recognize him. he came to that which was his own, but his own did not receive him. Yet to all who received him, to those who believed in his name, he gave the right to become children of God—children born not of natural descent, nor of human decision or a husband's will, but born of God. — JOHN 1:9-13, C AD 26

WILLIAM HOLMAN HUNT (1827-1910)

The Light of the World

Keble College, Oxford, UK/Bridgeman Art Library

Hunt shows Christ knocking on the door of mankind. Light emanates from Christ and also from his lantern. Looking toward Christ's feet, you see he is about to trample the apple representing the original sin.

OLD TESTAMENT PROPHECY

The Lord says to my Lord: "Sit at my right hand until I make your enemies a footstool for your feet." — PSALMS 110:1

NEW TESTAMENT FULFILLMENT

The Son is the radiance of God's glory and the exact representation of his being, sustaining all things by his powerful word. After he had provided purification for sins, he sat down at the right hand of the Majesty in heaven. — HEBREWS 1:3, C AD 33

After the Lord Jesus had spoken to them, he was taken up into heaven and he sat at the right hand of God. — MARK 16:19, C AD 33

God has raised this Jesus to life, and we are all witnesses of the fact. Exalted to the right hand of God, he has received from the Father the promised Holy Spirit and has poured out what you now see and hear. For David did not ascend to heaven, and yet he said,

"The Lord said to my Lord:
Sit at my right hand
until I make your enemies
a footstool for your feet."— ACTS 2:32-35, C AD 33

DIEGO RODRIGUEZ DE SILVA Y VELASQUEZ (1599-1660)

Coronation of the Virgin, 1641-1644

Prado, Madrid, Spain/Bridgeman Art Library

Velasquez has given such extraordinary attention to these figures, the painting itself is a heavenly spectacle. Christ has indeed taken his rightful place at the right hand of God. Holding a scepter in one hand, he aids God in crowning the Virgin Mary. God grasps the universe in his left hand. Mary has ascended with the assistance of an assembly of angels. The dove of the Holy Ghost bathes this glorious event with a luminous glow.

THE DISCIPLES WERE TOLD THEY WOULD BE HATED; THEY WOULD ALSO RECEIVE GREAT REWARDS

Then you will be handed over to be persecuted and put to death, and you will be hated by all nations because of me. — MATTHEW 24:9, C AD 33

Twelve men followed Jesus as apostles. One, knowing he betrayed the Son of God, killed himself. The other eleven continued to preach of Jesus as the Messiah of the Old Testament, in spite of the persecutions and hardships they suffered.

All the disciples were eventually killed for their faith, except John who died of old age after writing The Book of Revelation. The faith held by these men is a strong testimony that Jesus is the true Son of God, and that all the details of his life, death, and resurrection are true.

We did not follow cleverly invented stories when we told you about the power and coming of our Lord Jesus Christ, but we were eyewitnesses to his Majesty. — 2 PETER 1:16, C AD 66

Peter said to him, "We have left everything to follow you!" "I tell you the truth," Jesus replied, "no one who has left home or brothers or sisters or mother or father or children or fields for me and the gospel will fail to receive a hundred times as much in this present age (homes, brothers, sisters, mothers, children and fields—and with them, persecutions) and in the age to come, eternal life. But many who are first will be last, and the last first." — MARK 10:28-31, C AD 33

DOMENICO GHIRLANDAIO (1448-1494)

Calling of Peter and Andrew

Sistine Chapel, Vatican Palace, Vatican State. Scala/Art Resource, NY

This verdant waterside setting is the Sea of Galilee. Christ was walking along the shore when he happened upon Simon Peter and Andrew, who are kneeling on the right. He invited them to follow him and they became his first disciples. The boat behind Christ at first glance recalls its representation of the church. Ghirlandaois' depiction is twofold: in the boat are James and John, who became Christ's third and fourth disciples.

OLD TESTAMENT PROPHECY

Nevertheless, there will be no more gloom for those who were in distress. In the past he humbled the land of Zebulun and the land of Naphtali, but in the future he will honor Galilee of the Gentiles, by the way of the sea, along the Jordan. — ISAIAH 9:1, C 734 BC

NEW TESTAMENT FULFILLMENT

Then Jesus began to denounce the cities in which most of his miracles had been performed, because they did not repent. "Woe to you, Korazin! Woe to you, Bethsaida! If the miracles that were performed in you had been performed in Tyre and Sidon, they would have repented long ago in sackcloth and ashes. But I tell you, it will be more bearable for Tyre and Sidon on the day of judgment than for you. And you, Capernaum, will you be lifted up to the skies? No, you will go down to the depths. If the miracles that were performed in you had been performed in Sodom, it would have remained to this day." — MATTHEW 11:20-23, C AD 31

So completely were these cities destroyed that there still remains some doubt as to the exact location of Bethsaida and Chorazin. E. Ewing says of Chorazin in the INTERNATIONAL STANDARD BIBLE ENCYCLOPEDIA, *"It must have been a place of some importance, and highly privileged by the ministry of Jesus. It was already deserted in the time of Eusebius, who places it two miles from Capernaum. We can hardly doubt that it is represented by the extensive ruins of Kerazeh. . . . It is utterly desolate: a few carved stones being seen among the heaps." The same author says of Bethsaida, "The site (of its ruins) is still uncertain, but most probably was near the southeast corner of the wide plain, about a mile and a half from where the Jordan enters the Sea of Galilee." Capernaum was so completely "brought down to Hades" that its exact location was not known until the First World War, when some German monks, who were put in a concentration camp near the Sea of Galilee for the duration, discovered the site of the ancient city. Until that time maps of Palestine usually gave two possible locations for Capernaum.* —FROM CHRIST THE PROPHET BY FRED JOHN MELDAU

JUAN CORREA DE VIVAR (1510-C. 1561)

The Prophet Isaiah

Museo de Santa Cruz, Toledo, Spain/Bridgeman Art Library

Juan Correa de Vivar has depicted Isaiah with a far more regal stature than many other artists have. The rich folds of his cloak bring to mind the fluidity and eloquence of his writing style.

165

The apostle Paul began as a persecutor of those who believed in Christ. Dramatically he turned to a faith in Jesus, providing a persuasive testimony of the Messiahship of Yeshua. Paul was, no doubt, one of the most zealous and learned Jews of his time. In his zeal he became the most notorious persecutor of the believers. He dragged many of them in chains to prison for their faith. Then suddenly, a dramatic experience released him from his own spiritual chains. He accepted Jesus as the Messiah and became the most devout follower and the greatest propagator of the faith. He carried the message throughout the world, and when the message became so powerful as to threaten the Roman Empire, he died for the Messiah in whom he had come to believe.

Paul, a servant of Christ Jesus, called to be an apostle and set apart for the gospel of God—the gospel he promised beforehand through his prophets in the Holy Scriptures regarding his Son, who as to his human nature was a descendant of David, and who through the Spirit of holiness was declared with power to be the Son of God by his resurrection from the dead: Jesus Christ our Lord.

Through him and for his name's sake, we received grace and apostleship to call people from among all the Gentiles to the obedience that comes from faith. And you also are among those who are called to belong to Jesus Christ. — ROMANS 1:1-6, C AD 60

I ask then: Did God reject his people? By no means! I am an Israelite myself, a descendant of Abraham, from the tribe of Benjamin. God did not reject his people, whom he foreknew.
— ROMANS 11:1, C AD 60

CARAVAGGIO (1573-1610)

Conversion of Saint Paul, 1600

S. Maria del Popolo, Rome, Italy. Scala/Art Resource, NY

Blinded by a vision unseen by those around him, Paul falls from his horse. This vision was the calling of the Lord. Previously, we saw how Caravaggio utilized dramatic lighting to portray the enlightenment of Thomas. This scene is bathed with the same intense light, signifying Paul's revelation.

JESUS PREDICTS THE TEMPLE WILL BE DESTROYED
AND NOT ONE STONE WILL REMAIN ATOP ANOTHER

Jesus left the temple and was walking away when his disciples came up to him to call his attention to its buildings. "Do you see all these things?" he asked. "I tell you the truth, not one stone here will be left on another; every one will be thrown down." — MATTHEW 24:1-2, C AD 33-37

These days shall come that thine enemies… shall lay thee even with the ground, and thy children within thee; and they shall not leave in thee one stone upon another; because thou knewest not the time of thy visitation. — LUKE 19:43-44, C AD 33

The Temple was a glorious, world-famous structure with abundant gold throughout. The walls surrounding the Temple and the Temple itself were made of huge stones, some sixty feet long by eight feet high and up to ten feet thick, even smaller stones weighing thousands of pounds. To say that every stone would be removed from the other was beyond belief, but Jesus said it and it did happen. After months of siege, and violent fighting, the Roman general Titus was loathe to give the command to destroy the Temple. In fact, when the city was finally put to the torch, Titus commanded that the Temple be spared. But One greater than Titus had spoken, and the Temple was put to flames by a soldier who threw a torch into it. The intense heat caused the molten gold to run down between the stones and down to the foundations. The avaricious Romans tore the Temple down, stone by stone, to recover the gold, as reported by John Fred Meldau.

The destruction of the Temple was well documented by the Jewish officer Flavius Josephus. He was captured by the Romans but was employed while a prisoner under General Titus to record the siege of the Temple. He wrote about the histories of the Jewish people and the destruction of Jerusalem and the Temple which documented the fulfillment of Jesus' prophecy. The Temple was destroyed in 70 A.D.

JAMES JACQUES JOSEPH TISSOT (1836-1902)

Jerusalem, Jerusalem, and Jesus Wept; Illustrations for "The Life of Christ," c. 1886-1896
(gouache on paperboard)

Brooklyn Museum of Art, New York, USA/Bridgeman Art Library

The top painting shows Jesus preaching in the Temple; in the bottom painting he cries because of the eventual destruction of the city.

169

As he approached Jerusalem and saw the city, he wept over it and said, "If you, even you, had only known on this day what would bring you peace—but now it is hidden from your eyes. The days will come upon you when your enemies will build an embankment against you and encircle you and hem you in on every side. They will dash you to the ground, you and the children within your walls. They will not leave one stone on another, because you did not recognize the time of God's coming to you." — LUKE 19:41-44, C AD 33

An Embankment or Rampart or Palisade

"Palisade" is a military term, indicating a defensive trench and wall, with stakes set in it at an angle. It is most amazing that Titus used this particular type of embankment. It seemed unnecessary and his chief men advised against it. Yet Titus built a trench and palisade about Jerusalem, five miles in circumference, exactly as Christ said he would. Josephus [writing in THE WARS OF THE JEWS*] describes the circuit and adds, "all hope of [the Jews] escaping was now cut off. . . together with their liberty of going out of the city." Here is another amazing fact: The garrison inside of Jerusalem was ten times the number of the besiegers, and yet the city fell. Titus himself commented, "We have certainly had God for our helper in this war. It is God who ejected the Jews out of these fortifications. For what could the hands of men, or any machines, do towards throwing down such fortifications?" —* THE MESSIAH IN BOTH TESTAMENTS, *BY* FRED JOHN MELDAU

The Sack of Jerusalem in 70 A.D.
Detail from the Arch of Titus, c. 81 A.D.
Forum, Rome, Italy/Index/Bridgeman Art Gallery

This detail is taken from a grand arch erected in Titus' name after the destruction of Jerusalem. We see the soldiers looting the treasures of the temple, including a large menorah.

GREAT TRIBULATIONS AND WOES WOULD ACCOMPANY THE SIEGE AND DESTRUCTION OF JERUSALEM

According to Fred John Meldau, "the attackers came at the Passover season, when nearly three million Jews are estimated to have been in the city. Before long the famine in the city became so severe that hunger drove men to eat sandals, leather girdles, and straw. About 1,300,000 Jews perished in the siege and 130,000 were slain when the city capitulated, and 97,000 of the survivors were then sold into slavery." No wonder Jesus cried. He knew the destiny of the Jewish people.

In 70 A.D., after the fall of Jerusalem and the destruction of the temple, the Jewish people who survived were sold as slaves to most nations of the world.

They will fall by the sword and will be taken as prisoners to all the nations. Jerusalem will be trampled on by the Gentiles until the times of the Gentiles are fulfilled. — LUKE 21:24, C AD 33

A brief history of Jerusalem:
70 A.D. to 637 A.D. — Jerusalem under the Roman Emperor
637 — The Saracen (Islamic) conquest of the Holy Land
1099 — The Crusaders took the city
1187 — Saladin, Sultan of Egypt and Syria, took control
1517 — Jerusalem became part of the Turkish Empire
1917 — Great Britain conquered Jerusalem, ending Turkish rule
1967 — Israel took Jerusalem back

An attempt was made to change God's word. According to Fred John Meldau, "Julian the Apostate once tried to nullify this prophecy, by giving the Jews permission to rebuild the temple. He donated vast sums of money toward this project—but it failed. Gibbon, the Roman historian who had no love for Christianity, wrote of this endeavor: 'An earthquake, a whirlwind, and a fiery eruption which overturned and scattered the new foundations of the Temple.' The Jews then abandoned their ill-advised effort to rebuild their temple." This image shows the temple and the huge wall that surrounds it. It appears that Titus is assembling his army for attack.

The Destruction of Jerusalem in 70 A.D., engraved by Louis Haghe (1806-1885);
lithograph by David Roberts (1796-1864) (after)

Private Collection/The Stapleton Collection/Bridgeman Art Library

JERUSALEM WILL BE PLOWED OVER

OLD TESTAMENT PROPHECY

Therefore because of you, Zion will be plowed like a field. Jerusalem will become a heap of rubble, the temple hill a mound overgrown with thickets. — MICAH 3:12, C 430 BC

HISTORICAL FULFILLMENT

Terentus Rufus, who was in charge of the Roman army left in Jerusalem commanded that the temple area be plowed over. "The Wailing Wall," which remains to this day, was part of the wall around the temple compound, not part of the temple itself.

ANDRE BEAUNEVEU (C. 1335-1403/13)

Fr. 13091 f.29v The prophet Micah (manuscript) Psalter of Jean, Duke of Berry (c. 1386)

Biblioteque Nationale, Paris, France/Bridgeman Art Library

Micah prophesied under Kings Ahez and Hezekiah of Judah. Beauneveu portrays Micah sitting on a seat of prominence, possibly where he wrote the prophesy on Jerusalem.

Eponet
dominus
donnnes
iniquitates nostras.

outes nos
iniquitates
nostra.

Flavius Josephus was a soldier and historian born in A.D. 37. Josephus was drafted into the Jewish revolutionary forces to fight Rome and was captured by the Romans. But because of his skill as a writer, Titus called upon him to record the history of the battle to take the Holy Temple. His writing is one of the only sources of what happened during this time other than the Bible. Four works of Josephus survive to this day and are available as a history of the time.

In JEWISH ANTIQUITIES, *published in 93 A.D., Josephus wrote the following, here as translated by William Whiston: "Now there was about this time Jesus, a wise man, if it be lawful to call him a man; for he was a doer of wonderful works, a teacher of such men as receive the truth with pleasure. He drew over to him both many of the Jews and many of the Gentiles. He was [the] Christ. And when Pilate, at the suggestion of the principal men amongst us, had condemned him to the cross, those that loved him at the first did not forsake him; for he appeared to them alive again the third day; as the divine prophets had foretold these and ten thousand other wonderful things concerning him. And the tribe of Christians, so named from him, are not extinct at this day."*

Beginning in the 17th century, some cast doubt on the authenticity of this passage from Josephus. Recent scholarship has proved that much of the passage is original. See "The Coincidences of the Testimonium of Josephus and the Emmaus Narrative of Luke," by G. J. Goldberg.

Frontispiece to The Works of Flavius Josephus, 1725 (engraving)
(b/w photo) by English School (18th Century)
Private Collection/Bridgeman Art Library

The works of Flavius Josephus have been translated and published by many scholars. The frontispiece of this version depicts the importance of the Jewish ceremonial garments, from the type of material they are made from to how they are made, and how they were to be worn.

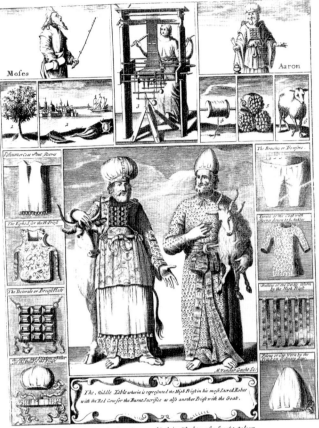

Moses

Aaron

Columns or Pillars

The Breeches or Drawers

The Ephod for the H. Priest

Tunica of the Priest with Sleeves down to the Ankles

The Pectorale or Breastplate

Lining of the Mitre Worn by the High Priest

Colour of Cap Worn by the Priests or Plain Linen

H. Vander Gucht Sc.

The Middle Table wherein is represented the High Priest in his most Sacred Robes with the Red Cow for the Burnt Sacrifice as also another Priest with the Goat.

1 *COCCUS a Shrub bearing a berry used in dying Wool &c. of a Scarlet Colour*

2 { *Hyacinthus a deep Blew used in Dying Woolalone. Purpura a Shelfish found on the Seaside near Tyre used in dying a Crimson Colour.*

3 *The manner of Wearing Cloath used by the Antients.*

4 *Gold Wire Weaved or wrought in the Sacred Vestments.*

5 *Flax for linnen Garments*

6 *Wool for outward Garments*

Page 177.

THE
WORKS
OF
Flavius Josephus:

Translated into English

By Sir *ROGER L'ESTRANGE*, Knight.

VIZ.

I. The Antiquities of the *Jews*, in twenty Books.
II. Their Wars with the *Romans*, in Seven Books.
III. The Life of JOSEPHUS written by himself.
IV. His Book against *Apion*, in Defence of the Antiquities of the *Jews*, in Two Parts.
V. The Martyrdom of the *Maccabees*. As also;
VI. *Philo*'s Embassy from the *Jews* of *Alexandria* to *Caius Caligula*.

All carefully revis'd, and compar'd with the original Greek.

To which are added,

Two Discourses, and several Remarks and Observations upon *JOSEPHUS*.

Together with

MAPS, SCULPTURES, and Accurate INDEXES.

The Fourth EDITION, with the Addition of a new Map of *Palæstine*, the Temple of *Jerusalem*, and the Genealogy of *Herod* the Great; taken from *Villalpandus, Reland, &c.*

LONDON,

Printed for the Executors of R. SARE: And sold by J. DARBY, A. BETTESWORTH, F. FAYRAM, J. PEMBERTON, C. RIVINGTON, J. HOOKE, F. CLAY, J. BATLEY, E. SYMON, and R. WILLIAMSON, MDCCXXV.

ISRAEL, A NATION BORN IN A DAY

Almost three thousand years ago, Isaiah told of Jewish people returning to the "promised" land in a day.

OLD TESTAMENT PROPHECY

Who has ever heard of such a thing? Who has ever seen such things? Can a country be born in a day or a nation be brought forth in a moment? Yet no sooner is Zion in labor than she gives birth to her children. — ISAIAH 66:8, C 690 BC

In a vote of the United Nations, Isaiah's prophecy was fulfilled and Israel became a nation on May 14, 1948. Israel was born in a day. The time of the Gentiles is almost fulfilled and the Jewish people are back in Israel.

RAPHAEL (RAFFAELLO SANZIO OF URBINO) (1483-1520)

The Prophet Isaiah, 1511-1512

S. Agostino, Rome, Italy. Scala/Art Resource, NY

One glimpse at Raphael's Isaiah and it is easy to see similarities with Michelangelo's Moses. Isaiah quickly turns in urgency, as if caught off guard by a new vision, new prophecy. Rather than the Ten Commandments, he holds the scroll bearing his prophecies of Christ's coming. His weight is shifted to one leg, as the other bare leg is uncovered—right at the precise moment he is about to leap to his feet.

THE JEWISH PEOPLE ARE SCATTERED THROUGHOUT THE WORLD AND THEN REGATHERED

For the land will be deserted by them and will enjoy its sabbaths while it lies desolate without them. They will pay for their sins because they rejected many laws and abhorred my decrees. Yet in spite of this, when they are in the land of their enemies, I will not reject them or abhor them so as to destroy them completely, breaking my covenant with them. I am the Lord their God.
— LEVITICUS 26:43-44, C 1450 BC

For I will take you from among the heathen, and gather you out of all countries, and will bring you into your own land. — EZEKIEL 36: 24-28, C 593 BC

What an amazing prophecy. The Jewish people were defeated first by the Babylonians and then when the Romans conquered them in 70 A.D. For almost two thousand years those who survived lived in over seventy different countries. God promised not to reject them and never to allow them to be destroyed completely as a people. The Jewish people, like no other in the world, have maintained their traditions and national identity while longing for the time when they could return to the Promised Land.

They will fall by the sword and will be taken as prisoners to all the nations. Jerusalem will be trampled on by the Gentiles until the times of the Gentiles are fulfilled. — LUKE 21:24. C AD 33

MICHELANGELO BUONARROTI (1475-1564)

The Prophet Ezekiel, 1510

Sistine Chapel, Vatican Palace, Vatican State. Scala/Art Resource, NY

Ezekiel appears as the most disconcerted of Michelangelo's prophets. His body sharply twists to the right. He wears an expression of utter astonishment on his face. His gestures mimic the startling emotions caused from his great vision.

OLD TESTAMENT PROPHECIES

Then the Lord your God will restore your fortunes and have compassion on you and gather you again from all the nations where he scattered you. Even if you have been banished to the most distant land under the heavens, from there the Lord your God will gather you and bring you back. He will bring you to the land that belonged to your fathers, and you will take possession of it. He will make you more prosperous and numerous than your fathers. — DEUTERONOMY 30:3-5, C 1410 BC

He will raise a banner for the nations and gather the exiles of Israel; he will assemble the scattered people of Judah from the four quarters of the earth. — ISAIAH 11:12, C 734 BC

The Jewish people although scattered and separated from each other, are yet miraculously preserved as one distinct people. Many of the Jewish people who didn't return home helped those who did by sending money, supplies, whatever they could.

MELOZZO DA FORLI (1438-1494)

Christ in Glory, 15th century

Palazzo del Quirinale, Rome, Italy. Scala/Art Resource, NY

In da Forli's painting, all the scattered people have assembled around the magnificent presence of Christ. His pull is like that of gravity, naturally drawing his followers to him.

OPVS · MELOTTII · FOROLIVIENSIS
QVI · SVMMOS · FORNICES · PINGENDI · ARTEM
MIRIS · OPTICAE · LEGIBVS
VEL · PRIMVS · INVENIT · VEL · ILLVSTRAVIT
EX · ABSIDE · VETERIS · TEMPLI · SS · XII · APOSTOLORVM
HVC · TRANSLATVM · ANNO · SAL · MDCCXI

Tens of thousands of Russian Jews are released to return, after hundreds of years, to their homeland.

OLD TESTAMENT PROPHECIES

I will say to the north, "Give them up!" and to the south, "Do not hold back. Bring my sons from afar and my daughters from the ends of the earth." — ISAIAH 43:6, C 690 BC

"However, the days are coming," declares the Lord, "when men will no longer say, 'As surely as the Lord lives, who brought the Israelites up out of Egypt,' but they will say, 'As surely as the Lord lives, who brought the Israelites up out of the land of the north and out of all the countries where he had banished them.' For I will restore them to the land I gave their forefathers."
— JEREMIAH 16:14-15, C 610 BC

For I will take you out of the nations; I will gather you from all the countries and bring you back into your own land. I will sprinkle clean water on you, and you will be clean; I will cleanse you from all your impurities and from all your idols. I will give you a new heart and put a new spirit in you; I will remove from you your heart of stone and give you a heart of flesh. And I will put my Spirit in you and move you to follow my decrees and be careful to keep my laws. You will live in the land I gave your forefathers; you will be my people, and I will be your God. — EZEKIEL 36:24-28, C 586 BC

MICHELANGELO BUONARROTI (1475-1564)

The Prophet Jeremiah, 1511
Sistine Chapel, Vatican Palace, Vatican State. Scala/Art Resource, NY

One glace at Michelangelo's Jeremiah and we immediately recall Auguste Rodin's *The Thinker*. Jeremiah sits, face in hand, in purposeful contemplation.

OLD TESTAMENT PROPHECIES

There are to be twelve stones, one for each of the names of the sons of Israel, each engraved like a stele with the names of one of the twelve tribes. — EXODUS 28:21, C 1450 BC

In that day the Lord will reach out his hand a second time to reclaim the remnant that is left of his people from Assyria, from Lower Egypt, from Upper Egypt, from Cush, from Elam, from Babylonia, from Hamath, and from the islands of the sea. — ISAIAH 11:11, C 734 BC

From beyond the rivers of Cush my worshipers, my scattered people, will bring me offerings.—ZEPHANIAH 3:10, C 630 BC

This is what the Sovereign Lord says: "I will take the Israelites out of the nations where they have gone. I will gather them from all around and bring them back into their own land." — EZEKIEL 37:21, C 586 BC

It is believed that members of all twelve tribes migrated to Ethiopia (Cush) during the reign of King Solomon.

From 1989 to 1991, over 85,000 Ethiopian Jews known as Falashas flew home to Israel.

Twelve Tribes of Israel (engraving)
Private Collection/Bridgeman Art Library

This engraving represents the twelve tribes originating from the twelve sons of Jacob: Reuben, Simeon, Levi, Judah, Issachar, Zebulun, Gad, Asher, Benjamin, Dan, Naphtali, and Joseph (Ephraim and Manasseh).

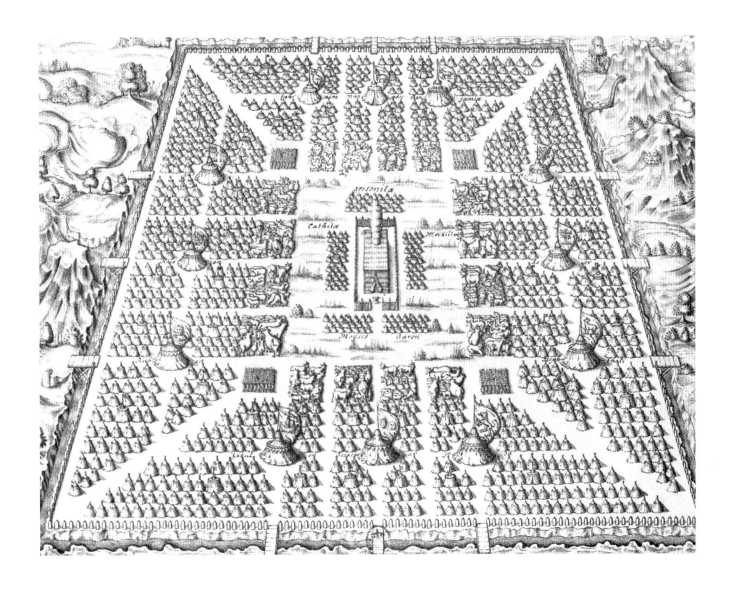

THE RETURN OF THE JEWS TO ISRAEL TRIGGERS BITTER CONFLICT

See how your enemies are astir, how your foes rear their heads. With cunning they conspire against your people; they plot against those you cherish. "Come," they say, "let us destroy them as a nation, that the name of Israel be remembered no more." With one mind they plot together; they form an alliance against you—the tents of Edom and the Ishmaelites, of Moab and the Hagrites, Gebal, Ammon and Amalek, Philistia, with the people of Tyre. Even Assyria has joined them to lend strength to the descendants of Lot. — PSALM 83:2-8

King David predicted almost three thousand years ago that the Jewish state would be surrounded by enemies. Israel is now surrounded by people who have at times united against her. Many wars and conflicts have occurred since 1948.

Psalms: frontispiece showing King David playing the lyre (printed book)
Nuremberg Bible (Biblia Sacra Germanaica), 1483
Private Collection/Bridgeman Art Library

We see a quite common appearance of David with his harp as he is composing the Psalms. The boat floating behind David is a foreshadowing symbol of the Church to be built by Christ. The dove of the Holy Ghost descends to speak to David, instructing him on writing his masterworks, a collection of which appear in the book shelf behind him.

Mein brüder waren gut vñ groß.vnd dē herrē was nit ein wolgeuallen in in . Ich bin außgegangen.vñ entgegen kumē dē heydē philisteo. Vnd hab außgezogen das schwert von seiner

verlaßen.werdē verleitet.Vñ dy vbergeschrift ditz psalms ist.8 psalm Dauid.

Nocturn an dem suntag.

Beatus vir qui.   Der erst psalm.

Elig ist der mann der nicht abtieng in dē

sen.vñ alle dig dy er wirdt thun werdē gelucksā O ir vngütigē nit also nit also.aber als d stauß dē der wind verwürfft võ dē antlytz der erde

Then the survivors from all the nations that have attacked Jerusalem will go up year after year to worship the King, the Almighty, and to celebrate the Feast of Tabernacles.

— ZECHARIAH 14:16, C 487 BC

In 1967 the Israeli Army recaptured Jerusalem and the Temple Mount in the Six Day War. When the Israelis won the Six Day War, they regained control of the Temple site for the first time in almost two thousand years. This small country defeated its large enemies only with God's help. Now Jews, Christians, and Muslims can worship in the Holy City.

This intense, passionate love for the Old City of Jerusalem was expressed in a published appeal by the Chief Rabbi of Palestine, Dr. Isaac Herzog, at the time the United Nations partitioned Palestine and "internationalized" the Old City of Jerusalem, finally putting it under the control of the Kingdom of Jordan. We quote from Dr. Herzog's appeal: "For millions of Jews the only glimmer of hope in their lives, embittered by appalling economic distress and utterly darkened by relentless persecution, has been the future national home. The climax of the shock is reached when we see Jerusalem—inexpressibly dear to every Jewish heart— cut out of the proposed Jewish dwarf state. On the banks of the rivers of Babylon our forefathers solemnly swore: 'If I forget thee, O Jerusalem, let my right hand forget her cunning.'...We close every Passover service and the most solemn service on the Day of Atonement with the exclamation: 'Next year in Jerusalem.' The Jewish mind is focused on that magic name 'YERUSHALAYIM'."

FOUQUET, JEAN (C.1420-1481)

Construction of the Temple of Jerusalem under the order of Solomon

Ms.247,f.163v. Giraudon/Art Resource

Center stage is the main construction of the Temple. Across the street from there, two people peer out over a balcony. They are Solomon and the Queen of Sheba. "When the queen of Sheba saw all the wisdom of Solomon and the palace he had built, the food on his table, the seating of his officials, the attending servants in their robes, his cupbearers, and the burnt offerings he made at the Temple of the Lord, she was overwhelmed." (I Kings 10:4-6)

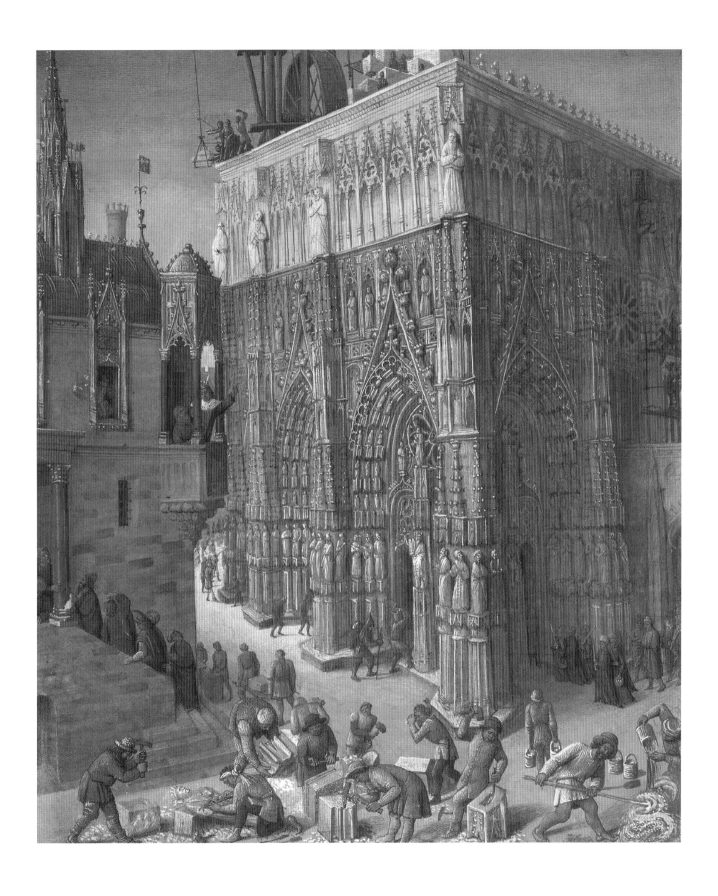

OLD TESTAMENT PROPHECY

Then will I purify the lips of the peoples, that all of them may call on the name of the Lord and serve him shoulder to shoulder. — ZEPHANIAH 3:9, C 630 BC

The language of Hebrew had ceased to be the common spoken language of the Jews. Eliazar ben Yehuda is certainly the only person in history who has restored an ancient language single-handedly. He began working earlier in this century in Palestine under the British Mandate to revive the dead language of Hebrew. That language made it possible for Jews to communicate with one another when Jewish people returned to Israel from seventy different nations.

THOMAS COOPER GOTCH

Alleluia

Exhi. 1896. Tate Gallery, London, Great Britain. Tate Gallery, London/Art Resource, NY

Gotch shows a chorus of different ages and cultures joining in song in a single language.

NEW TESTAMENT FULFILLMENT

Now learn this lesson from the fig tree: As soon as its twigs get tender and its leaves come out, you know that summer is near. Even so, when you see all these things, you know that it is near, right at the door. I tell you the truth, this generation will certainly not pass away until all these things have happened. Heaven and earth will pass away, but my words will never pass away.

— MATTHEW 24:32-35, C AD 33

In the Old Testament, the fig tree is a symbol of the Nation of Israel. For many years the fig tree showed no life. Then its twigs became tender and its leaves began to bud and spring forth.

PETRUS CHRISTUS (D. 1472)

Our Lady of the Barren Tree, c. 1444-1462 (oil on panel)

Thyssen-Bornemisza Collection, Madrid, Spain/Bridgeman Art Library

Mary and the infant Jesus are shown in a barren fig tree representing Israel.

195

B ut what about you?" he asked. "Who do you say I am?" Simon Peter answered, "You are the Christ, the Son of the living God." Jesus replied, "Blessed are you, Simon son of Jonah, for this was not revealed to you by man, but by my Father in heaven. And I tell you that you are Peter, and on this rock I will build my church, and the gates of Hades will not overcome it.
— MATTHEW 16:15-18, C AD 32

And this gospel of the kingdom will be preached in the whole world as a testimony to all nations. — MATTHEW 24:14, C AD 33

The Spectacular Growth of the Christian Church

Missionaries are now in almost every country of the world, even the most remote.
1430—one person in 99 of the world's population was a Christian.
1790—one person in 49 of the world's population is a Christian.
1940—one person in 32 of the world's population is a Christian.
1970—one person in 19 of the world's population is a Christian.
1980—one person in 16 of the world's population is a Christian.
1983—one person in 13 of the world's population is a Christian.
1986—one person in 11 of the world's population is a Christian.
1997—one person in 10 of the world's population is a Christian.

—FROM THE LAUSANNE STATISTICS TASK FORCE ON EVANGELISM

PALATINE SCHOOL OF AACHEN

The Four Evangelists
From the Treasury Gospels, fol. 14v. Carolingian, early 9th century
Cathedral Treasury, Palatine Chapel, Aachen, Germany. D.Y./Art Resource, NY

The writings of the four evangelists have contributed greatly to the spread of the Word. In this work we see all four evangelists, sitting at their desks and accompanied by the attributes Ezekiel prophesied. In the upper left hand corner is Matthew, a winged man inspired by an angel. In the lower left hand corner is Mark represented by a lion. In the upper right hand corner John is portrayed by an eagle and Luke is represented by the ox.

THE SPARSE DESERTS WILL BECOME FERTILE AND ISRAEL WILL BE RESTORED AS A LAND OF MILK AND HONEY

OLD TESTAMENT PROPHECIES

In days to come Jacob will take root, Israel will bud and blossom and fill all the world with fruit. — ISAIAH 27:6, C 730 BC

The desert and the parched land will be glad; the wilderness will rejoice and blossom. Like the crocus, it will burst into bloom; it will rejoice greatly and shout for joy. The glory of Lebanon will be give to it, the splendor of Carmel and Sharon. They will see the glory of the Lord, the splendor of our God. — ISAIAH 35:1-2, C 710 BC

The burning sand will become a pool, the thirsty ground bubbling springs. In the haunts where jackals once lay, grass and reeds and papyrus will grow. — ISAIAH 35:7, C 710 BC

FULFILLMENT

According to the United Nations Israel now has some of the most fertile land on earth, supplying citrus fruit to almost five hundred million Europeans. Implementation of irrigation systems has significantly increased the quality of the soil and the people of Israel have planted over two hundred million trees.

MICHELANGELO BUONARROTI (1475-1564)

The Prophet Isaiah, 1509

Sistine Chapel, Vatican Palace, Vatican State. Scala/Art Resource, NY

While reading, Isaiah has become distracted by a thought? a vision? Note the angel of inspiration on Isaiah's right shoulder.

PROPHECY

Jesus answered: "Watch out that no one deceives you. For many will come in my name, claiming, 'I am the Christ,' and will deceive many." — MATTHEW 24:4-5, C AD 33

. . . and many false prophets will appear and deceive many people. — MATTHEW 24:11, C AD 33

I am telling you now, before it happens, so that when it does happen you will believe that I am he. — JOHN 13:19, AD 33

You may say to yourselves, "How can we know when a message has not been spoken by the Lord? If what a prophet proclaims in the name of the Lord does not take place or come true that is a message the Lord has not spoken, that prophet has spoken presumptuously.
— DEUTERONOMY 18:21-22, C 1410 BC

FULFILLMENT

We have seen many false prophets since Jesus lived, but none has come even close to fulfilling the prophecies like Jesus, who fulfilled all prophecies, and no other "prophet" has maintained a following of believers both Jew and Gentile as Jesus has for two thousand years. Jesus has proven he is the true Son of God.

MATTHIAS GERUNG OR GEROU (C. 1500-68/70)

*'Beware of false prophets; they come to you with the garb of sheep but at heart they are ravenous wolves'
(Matthew 7 v.15, Luke 6 v.13), illustration of Christ's teaching,
section of wing panel from the Mompelgarter Altarpiece (panel)*
Kunsthistorisches Museum, Vienna, Austria/Bridgeman Art Library

The far left hand side of this illustration shows Christ as he is warning of the false prophets. Over his head hovers the Dove of the Holy Ghost inspiring his words. In Matthew 7:15-17 Christ states: "Watch out for false prophets. They come to you in sheep's clothing, but inwardly they are ferocious wolves. By their fruit you will recognize them. Do people pick grapes from thornbushes, or figs from thistles? Likewise every good tree bears good fruit, but a bad tree bears bad fruit." The tree in front of Christ bears the "good fruit" he speaks of. Continuing with Matthew 7:19, Christ says "Every tree that does not bear good fruit is cut down and thrown into the fire." As several people have gathered in the courtyard, we see a figure overlooking the crowd from the balcony. This is the proverbial wolf in sheep's clothing. Below him is a man carrying an ax to abolish the "bad tree" entering the piazza in the form of the seven-headed dragon.

Ringet darnach das ir durch die engen pforten ein geet / deñ die pfort
ist weyt vñ ð weg breyt / der da abfürt zur verdamnus / vnd iren
seind vil die dardurch geen / Vnd die pfort ist eng / vnd der weg
schmal / der da zům leben füret / vnd wenig ist ir die in finden. ꝛc.
Sehet euch fur vor den falschen propheten / die zů tuch kumen in
schaafs kleydern / inwendig aber seind es reyssend wölff / an
iren früchten solt ir sie erkennen / Mag man auch weintraubē
samlen von Dornen / vnd feygen von disteln / nein ꝛc. Also ei
ytlicher gütter boum / bringt gütte feucht / Aber
bösser fauler boum
bringt arge bösse
frucht :
ꝛc.

Math. 7.
Luc. 6. 13

OLD TESTAMENT PROPHECY

Those who are wise will shine like the brightness of the heavens, and those who lead many to righteousness, like the stars forever and ever. But you, Daniel, close up and seal the words of the scroll until the time of the end. Many will go here and there to increase knowledge.

— DANIEL 12:3-4, C 536 BC

Certainly the time we live in meets the description of Daniel's "time of the end." Just a casual reflection on modern travel, communications, and exponential increase in information in this computer age meets the requirements Daniel gives.

MICHELANGELO BUONARROTI (1475-1564)

The Prophet Daniel, 1511

Sistine Chapel, Vatican Palace, Vatican State. Scala/Art Resource, NY

All the prophets portrayed by Michelangelo are depicted as though inspired by angels. Daniel is no exception.

OLD TESTAMENT PROPHECY

Seventy "sevens" are decreed for your people and your holy city to finish transgression, to put an end to sin, to atone for wickedness, to bring in everlasting righteousness, to seal up vision and prophecy and to anoint the most holy. Know and understand this: From the issuing of the decree to restore and rebuild Jerusalem until the Anointed One, the ruler, comes, there will be seven "sevens," and sixty-two "sevens." It will be rebuilt with streets and a trench, but in times of trouble. After the sixty-two "sevens," the Anointed One will be cut off and will have nothing. The people of the ruler who will come will destroy the city and the sanctuary. — DANIEL 9:24-26, C 538 BC

NEW TESTAMENT FULFILLMENT

In those days Caesar Augustus issued a decree that a census should be taken of the entire Roman world. This was the first census that took place while Quirinius was governor of Syria. . . So Joseph also went . . . to Bethlehem. . . with Mary. While they were there, the time came for the baby to be born, and she gave birth to her firstborn, a son. She wrapped him in cloths and placed him in a manger, because there was no room for them in the inn. — LUKE 2:1-7, C 5 AD

To calculate the seventy weeks of years, we are directed to start with the command to rebuild Jerusalem (Daniel 9:25). This began in the seventh year of the reign of King Artaxerxes recorded in Ezra 7. (See Ezra 7:18, 25 and 9:9) This date is calculated at 458 B.C. The command to rebuild the city was reiterated by Artaxerxes in the twentieth year of his reign to Nehemiah (Nehemiah 2:1). Opposition had stopped the earlier attempts to rebuild.

Seven sevens equals forty-nine years, and sixty-two sevens equals 434 years. If you start at 458 B.C. and subtract 483 (49 + 434), you get 25 A.D. Daniel states the anointed one will be killed after this date. The prophet also says the Messiah must be cut off before the destruction of the temple. We know the date of the destruction of the temple to be 70 A.D. The Messiah had to die between 25 A.D. and 70 A.D. to fulfill the prophecy.

Christ was born approximately 6 B.C. to 4 B.C. during the reign of King Herod. (Historians tell us King Herod died in approximately 4 B.C.) The date of Jesus' death is estimated to be 27 A.D. to 29 A.D. Jesus is the anointed one of whom Daniel the prophet spoke.

GIAN LORENZO BERNINI (1598-1680)

Daniel, 17th century

S. Maria del Popolo, Rome, Italy. Scala/Art Resource, NY

B ecause of the increase in wickedness the love of most will grow cold. — MATTHEW 24:12

The twentieth century brought a rise in violence. Child abuse, rape and murder abound. According to R. J. Rummel, in his book DEATH BY GOVERNMENT, *34 million people have died fighting wars in the last century and an additional 170 million civilians have been massacred. In the closing years of the century between 170,000 and 230,000 Christians were martyred each year around the world. We have witnessed the fulfillment of the prophecy Jesus made two thousand years ago in our own time. Wickedness has increased and the love of many has grown cold.*

MICHELANGELO BUONARROTI (1475-1564)

Detail from The Original Sin and the Expulsion from Paradise, 1508-1512

Sistine Chapel, Vatican Palace, Vatican State. Scala/Art Resource, NY

Adam and Eve are driven out of the Garden of Eden for committing original sin.

There will be famines and earthquakes in various places. — MATTHEW 24:7, AD 33

When you hear of wars and revolutions, do not be frightened. These things must happen first, but the end will not come right away. There will be great earthquakes, famines, and pestilences in various places, and fearful events and great signs from heaven. — LUKE 21:9, 11, AD 33

In spite of huge advances in medical science, hunger and disease are global issues. Polio is cured and AIDS strikes with a vengeance. Famines still rage around the world, earthquakes are common. World relief agents rush from one disaster to another.

WILLIAM BLAKE (1757-1827)

Europe a Prophecy: Famine, 1794 (relief etching, engraving, watercolor)

Private Collection/Bridgeman Art Library, London

Blake shows the horror of famine.

I have spoken to you of earthly things and you do not believe; how then will you believe if I speak of heavenly things? No one has ever gone into heaven except the one who came from heaven—the Son of Man. Just as Moses lifted up the snake in the desert, so the son of Man must be lifted up, that everyone who believes in him may have eternal life. — JOHN 3:12-15

For God so loved the world that he gave his one and only Son, that whoever believes in him shall not perish but have eternal life. — JOHN 3:16

For God did not send his Son into the world to condemn the world, but to save the world through him. Whoever believes in him is not condemned, but whoever does not believe stands condemned already because he has not believed in the name of God's one and only Son. This is the verdict: Light has come into the world, but men loved darkness instead of light because their deeds were evil. Everyone who does evil hates the light, and will not come into light for fear that his deeds will be exposed. But whoever lives by the truth comes into the light, so that it may be seen plainly that what he has done has been done through God. — JOHN 3:17-21

God's love is fulfilled through Jesus' life, death, and resurrection.

MICHELANGELO BUONARROTI

(1475-1564)

Sistine Chapel ceiling: Creation of Adam, 1510 (fresco, post-restoration)
Vatican Museums and Galleries, Vatican City, Italy/Bridgeman Art Library

Michelangelo's famous painting of the creation of Adam shows God creating man in his image.

AFTERWORD

Of all the people on Earth, God chose the Jewish people to be the group from which the Messiah would come. God chose the patriarchs Abraham, Isaac and Jacob to be the line of heritage for Jesus. God then chose King David. Through the lineage of the patriarchs and King David, the world received the Messiah. Jesus, called Yeshua in the Hebrew Bible, was sent to the world through a virgin to fulfill what was said to Satan after man sinned in the Garden of Eden.

And I will put enmity between you and the woman, and between your offspring and hers, he will crush your head, and you will strike his heel. —GENESIS 3:15

God longed to be loved by the people He had created, but sin was in the way. Sin was removed when the Son of God underwent crucifixion. Sin could be forgiven because Jesus rose from the dead.

I tell you the truth, until heaven and earth disappear, not the smallest letter, not the least stroke of a pen, will by any means disappear from the Law until everything is accomplished.
— MATTHEW 5:18

The birth of Christ was prophesied in the Old Testament, as was His life, death, and resurrection. The Old Testament also prophesied the growth of the church and many other events that have occurred throughout the world over the last two thousand years, and are still occurring. As prophesied in the Old Testament, the Jewish people have suffered much but are now back in Israel, the holy land. Just as other prophecies have come true, so will these:

"I do not want you to be ignorant of this mystery, brothers, so that you may not be conceited: Israel has experienced a hardening in part until the full number of the Gentiles has come in."
And so all Israel will be saved, as it is written:
"The deliverer will come from Zion;
He will turn ungodliness away from Jacob.
And this is my covenant with them when I take away their sins." — ROMANS 11:25-27

For there is no difference between Jew and Gentile—the same Lord is Lord of all and richly blesses all who call on him, for, "Everyone who calls on the name of the Lord will be saved."—
ROMANS 10:12-13

Jesus did many other miraculous signs in the presence of his disciples, which are not recorded in this book. But these are written that you may believe that Jesus is the Christ, the Son of God, and that by believing you may have life in his name. — JOHN 20:30-31

The fulfillment of the Biblical prophecies is utterly fantastic, far beyond our ability to comprehend. Why should a man called Jesus be born and, knowing His fate, proceed to be betrayed, tortured, ridiculed, nailed to a cross, and, most amazingly and by far the hardest, be separated momentarily from God His father for no reason other than to save us from eternal damnation? Jesus could have declined his mission, as He says in Matthew 26:53-54: "Do you think I cannot call on my Father, and he will at once put at my disposal more than twelve legions of angels? But how then would the Scriptures be fulfilled that say it must happen in this way?" The full comprehension of this makes our hearts cry out and our eyes weep like those of a child with the fullness of knowing a love so great.

We award the Congressional Medal of Honor to a soldier who risks his life to save a comrade. What honor might we give to one who was willingly nailed to a cross and separated from his eternal spiritual home in the bosom of God in order to save the whole of mankind? The Messiah does not ask for a medal, only for your belief in Him. The disciples of Christ knew He was the Son of God. Without this belief, they would not have carried forth their ministry. Even Judas the betrayer had his role to play.

Lord, to whom shall we go? You have the words of eternal life. We believe and know that you are the Holy one of God. — JOHN 6:68-69

Then Jesus replied, "Have I not chosen you the twelve, yet one of you is a devil." He meant Judas. — JOHN 6:70-71

Heaven and earth will pass away; but my words will never pass away. —MATTHEW 24:35

Jesus knows all things.

We pray that those who turn the leaves of this book might ponder over the Bible as truly the Word of God written by men under the direction of the Holy Spirit, and that they might see the artists whose splendid works are shown here as inspired by the Holy Spirit. Such works of art have made it possible for many people, both those who could read and those who could not, to be inspired and to believe. We trust that they will convince people of the truth even today.

Oh, the depth of the riches of the wisdom and knowledge of God! How unsearchable his judgments, and his paths beyond tracing out! "Who has known the mind of the Lord? Or who has been his counselor?" "Who has ever given to God, that God should repay him?" For from him and through him and to him are all things. To him be the glory forever! Amen.— ROMANS 11:33-36

BIBLIOGRAPHY

"27 Prophecies Fulfilled in One Day." Chosen People Publications: Charlotte, NC, 1986.

"21 Reasons to Believe." Chosen People Ministries, Inc.: Charlotte, NC, 1986.

"It is Written and the Scripture was Fulfilled." The Society for Distributing Hebrew Scriptures: Middlesex, HA8 7LF, England, 1993.

"The Messiah of Israel." The Society for Distributing Hebrew Scriptures: Middlesex HA8 7LF, England, 1993.

Adams, Laurie Schneider. *Art Across Time, Volume I (Prehistory to the Fourteenth Century) and Volume II (The Fourteenth Century to the Present).* McGraw-Hill College, 1999.

Alley, Ronald. *Graham Sutherland.* Tate Gallery, London, 1982

Gardner, Helen. *Art Through The Ages.* Revised by Horst de la Croix and Richard G. Tansey, San Jose State University. Harcourt Brace Jovanovich, Inc: New York, Chicago, San Francisco, Atlanta, 1975.

Hall, James. *Dictionary of Subjects and Symbols in Art.* Icon Editions, Harper & Row: New York, Hagerstown, San Francisco, London., 1974, 1979.

Hartt, Frederick. *History of Italian Renaissance Art.* Prentice-Hall, Inc.: Englewood Cliffs, N.J. and Harry N. Abrams, Inc.: New York, 1969.

Janson, H. W. *History of Art.* Prentice-Hall, Inc.: Englewood Cliffs, N.J. and Harry N. Abrams, Inc., New York. 1962.

Jeffrey, Grant R. *Armageddon —Appointment with Destiny.* Frontier Research Publications: Toronto, Ontario m8z 5m4, 1997.

Meldau, Fred John. "Christ The Prophet." The Christian Victory Publishing Company: Denver, Co., 1957.

Meldau, Fred John. "Messiah in Both Testaments." The Christian Victory Publishing Company: Denver, Co., 1957.

Paoletti, John T. and Radke, Gary M. *Art in Renaissance Italy.* Prentice Hall: Upper Saddle River, NY, 1997.

Pelikan, Jaroslav. *The Illustrated Jesus through the Centuries.* Yale University Press: New Haven & London, 1997.

Snyder, James. *Northern Renaissance Art. Painting, Sculpture, The Graphic Arts from 1350 to 1575.* Prentice-Hall, Inc. and Harry N. Abrams, Inc. 1985.

Walvoord, John F. *Every Prophecy of the Bible.* "Formerly titled The Prophecy Knowledge Handbook." Chariot Publishing Co.: Colorado Springs, CO., 1990, 1999.

INDEX TO ARTWORKS

Abraham and Melchizedek (Dieric Bouts) 53
Abraham and the Three Angels 25
Adoration of the Magi (Albrecht Durer) 41
Adoration of the Magi (Gentile De Fabriano) 6, 8
Adoration of the Magi (Sandro Botticelli) 23
Adoration of the Mystic Lamb (Jan Van Eyck) 117
Adoration of the Shepherds (Hugo Van Der Goes) 39
Alleluia (Thomas Cooper Gotch) 193
Angelico, Fra, Raising of Lazarus 61; The Mocking of Christ 109; Crucifixion 123 Crucifixion with the Sponge-Bearer 131
Annunciation (Jan Van Eyck) 17
Arch of Titus 171
Ascension of Christ (Rembrandt Van Rijn) 157
Baptism of Christ (Pietro Perugino) 49
Barna Da Siena, The Elders Paying Judas 87; Kiss of Judas 89
Beauneveu, Andre, The Prophet Micah 175
Bernini, Gian Lorenzo, Daniel 205
Beware of false prophets; (Matthias Gerung) 201
Blake, William, Europe a Prophecy; Famine 209
Botticelli, Sandro, The Adoration of the Magi 23

Bouts, Dieric, Abraham and Melchizedek 53
Brunelleschi, Filippo, Sacrifice of Isaac 27
Buonarroti, Michelangelo, Pieta 151
Calling of Peter and Andrew (Domenico Ghirlandaio) 163
Calvary (Andrea Mantegna) 119, 121
Calvary (Maerten Van Heemskerck) 145
Caravaggio, The Doubting of St. Thomas 155; Conversion of St. Paul 167
Cassis, Louis Francis, Sepulchral Monument of the Kings of Judah 11
Chagall, Marc, Yellow Crucifixion 21
Christ at the Sea of Galilee (Jacopo Tintoretto) 55
Christ before Caiaphas (Giotto Di Bondone) 95
Christ before Pilate (Jacopo Tintoretto) 101
Christ before Pontius Pilate (Pietro Lorenzetti) 97
Christ Driving the Traders from the Temple (El Greco) 69
Christ Falls on the Way to Calvary (Raphael) 115
Christ in Glory (Melozzo Da Forli) 183
Christ Pantocrator 37
Christus, Petrus, Our Lady of the Barren Tree 195
Ciseri, Antonio, Ecco Homo 104
Construction of the Temple of Jerusalem Under the Order of Solomon (Jean Fouquet) 191

Conversion of St. Paul (Caravaggio)   167

Coronation of the Virgin (Diego Velasquez)   161

Correa De Vivar, Juan, The Prophet Isaiah   165

Cranach The Elder, Lucas, Crucifixion   137

Creation of Adam (Michelangelo)   211

Crivelli, Carlo, The Crucifixion   143

Crucifixion (Carlo Crivelli)   143

Crucifixion (El Greco)   127

Crucifixion (Fra Angelico)   123

Crucifixion (Graham Sutherland)   129

Crucifixion (Hubert Van Eyck)   125

Crucifixion (Lucas Cranach The Elder)   137

Crucifixion (Mathias Gruenewald)   135

Crucifixion (Peter Paul Rubens)   133

Crucifixion with the Sponge-Bearer (Fra Angelico)   131

Dali, Salvador, The Sacrament of the Last Supper   76

Daniel (Gian Lorenzo Bernini)   205

Darkness at Christ's Death (Limbourg Brothers)   139, 141

David (Michelangelo)   35

Dead Christ (Hans Holbein The Younger)   70

Descent From the Cross (Rosso Fiorentino)   147

Despoiling of Christ (El Greco)   107

Destruction of Jerusalem (David Roberts)   173

Disputation with the Doctors (Duccio Di Buoninsegna)   13

Doubting of St. Thomas (Follower of Caravaggio)   155

Duccio Di Buoninsegna, Disputation with the Doctors 13; Entry into Jerusalem 73; Flagellation of Christ   81

Dürer, Albrecht, Adoration of the Magi   41; Madonna of the Cherries   2

Ecco Homo (Antonio Ciseri)   104

El Greco, Christ Driving the Traders from the Temple 69; The Despoiling of Christ 107; Crucifixion   127

Elders Paying Judas (Barna Da Siena)   87

Entombment (Mathias Gruenewald)   111

Entombment (Peter Paul Rubens)   149

Entry into Jerusalem (Duccio Di Buoninsegna)   73

Entry of Christ into Jerusalem (Pietro Lorenzetti)   75

Europe a Prophecy; Famine (William Blake)   209

Fiorentino, Rosso, Descent From the Cross   147

Flagellation of Christ (Duccio Di Buoninsegna)   81

Flagellation of Christ (Jaime Huguet)   103

Flight into Egypt (Giotto Di Bondone)   45

Fouquet, Jean, Construction of the Temple of Jerusalem Under the Order of Solomon   191

Four Evangelists (Palatine School of Aachen)   197

Frontispiece to The Works of Flavius Josephus   177

Gentile De Fabriano, Nativity 6; The Adoration of the Magi   8

Gerung, Matthias, Beware of false prophets   201

Ghirlandaio, Domenico, Calling of Peter and Andrew   163

Giotto Di Bondone, The Flight into Egypt 45; Kiss of Judas 91;

Christ before Caiaphas   95

Gotch, Thomas Cooper, Alleluia   193

Gruenewald, Mathias, Entombment 111; Crucifixion   135

Holbein The Younger, Hans, Dead Christ   70

Huguet, Jaime, The Flagellation of Christ   103

Hunt, William Holman, The Light of the World   159

Isaac Blessing Jacob (Jusepe De Ribera)   28

Jan Van Hemessen, Parable of the Unmerciful Servant   56

Jerusalem, Jerusalem, Jesus Wept (James Jacques Joseph Tissot)   169

Jesus Healing the Blind of Jericho (Nicolas Poussin)   59

Jesus Wept (James Jacques Joseph Tissot)   169

Jusepe De Ribera, Isaac Blessing Jacob   28

Kiss of Judas (Barna De Siena)   89

Kiss of Judas (Giotto Di Bondone)   91

Last Supper (Cosimo Rosselli)   83

Last Supper (Leonardo Da Vinci)   79

Leonardo Da Vinci, The Virgin of the Rocks 19; The Last Supper   79

Let Him be Crucified (James Jacques Joseph Tissot)   99

Light of the World (William Holman Hunt)   159

Limbourg Brothers, Darkness at Christ's Death   139, 141

Lorenzetti, Pietro, Entry of Christ into Jerusalem 75; Christ before Pontius Pilate   97

Madonna of the Cherries (Albrecht Dürer)   2

Mantegna, Andrea, Calvary 119, 121; Resurrection of Christ   153

Martini, Simone, The Road to Calvary   113

Masaccio, The Tribute Money   66

Massacre of the Innocents (Guido Reni)   43

Melozzo Da Forli, Christ in Glory   183

Michelangelo, The Original Sin and the Expulsion from Paradise 15, 207; David 35; Moses 65; The Prophet Zaccariah 93; The Prophet Ezekiel 181; The Prophet Jeremiah 185; The Prophet Isaiah 199; The Prophet Daniel   203; The Creation of Adam 211

Mocking of Christ (Fra Angelico)   109

Moses (Michelangelo)   65

Original Sin and the Expulsion from Paradise (Michelangelo)   15, 207

Our Lady of the Barren Tree (Petrus Christus)   195

Palatine School of Aachen, The Four Evangelists   197

Parable of the Unmerciful Servant (Jan Van Hemessen)   56

Perugino, Pietro, The Baptism of Christ   49

Pieta (Michelangelo Buonarroti)   151

Poussin, Nicolas, The Summer of Ruth and Boaz 31; Jesus Healing the Blind of Jericho   59

Prophet Daniel (Michelangelo)   203

Prophet Ezekiel (Michelangelo)   181

Prophet Isaiah (Juan Correa De Vivar)   165

Prophet Isaiah (Michelangelo)   199

Prophet Isaiah (Raphael)   179

Prophet Jeremiah (Michelangelo)   185

Prophet Micah (Andre Beauneveu)   175

Prophet Zaccariah (Michelangelo)   93

Psalms: frontispiece showing King David playing the lyre   189

Raising of Lazarus (Fra Angelico)   61

Raphael, Christ Falls on the Way to Calvary 115; The Prophet
   Isaiah   179

Rembrandt Van Rijn, The Ascension of Christ   157

Reni, Guido, Massacre of the Innocents   43

Resurrection of Christ (Andrea Mantegna)   153

Road to Calvary (Simone Martini)   113

Roberts, David, The Destruction of Jerusalem   173

Rosselli, Cosimo, Last Supper   83

Rubens, Peter Paul, The Crucifixion 133; The Entombment
   149

Sacrament of the Last Supper (Salvador Dali)   76

Sacrifice of Isaac (Filippo Brunelleschi)   27

Saint John in the Desert (Domenico Veneziano)   47

Sepulchral Monument of the Kings of Judah (Louis Francis
   Cassis)   11

St. John the Forerunner   63

St. Joseph and Nicodemus (Michael Wolgemut)   85

Summer of Ruth and Boaz (Nicolas Poussin)   31

Sutherland, Graham, The Crucifixion   129

Tintoretto, Jacopo, Christ at the Sea of Galilee 55; Christ before
   Pilate   101

Tissot, James Jacques Joseph, Let Him be Crucified 99;
   Jerusalem, Jerusalem; Jesus Wept;   169

Tree of Jesse   33

Tribute Money (Masaccio)   66

Twelve Tribes of Israel   187

Van Der Goes, Hugo, Adoration of the Shepherds   39

Van Eyck, Hubert, The Crucifixion   125

Van Eyck, Jan, The Annunciation 17; Adoration of the Mystic
   Lamb   117

Van Heemskerck, Maerten, Calvary   145

Velasquez, Diego, Coronation of the Virgin   161

Veneziano, Domenico, Saint John in the Desert   47

Virgin of the Rocks (Leonardo Da Vinci)   19

Wolgemut, Michael, St. Joseph and Nicodemus   85

Yellow Crucifixion (Marc Chagall)   21